To Theresa,

Happy

Graduation!

Love,
Mimi

H. ALLEN SMITH

DON'T
GET PERCONEL
WITH A CHICKEN

STEIN AND DAY/*Publishers*/New York

First published in 1959

Copyright © 1957, 1959 by H. Allen Smith

A portion of the material in this book appeared originally in *Good Housekeeping*.

The items from *The New Yorker* on pages 14, 15, and 16, copyright © 1956, 1957, 1958 The New Yorker Magazine, Inc.

"Trouble" from ROARING GUNS by David Statler, copyright © 1938, by Simon and Shuster, Inc.

Excerpt from THE YOUNG VISITERS by Daisy Ashford, copyright 1919 by George H. Doran Co., reprinted by permission of Doubleday & Co., Inc. Canadian distribution by permission of Chatto and Windus.

Excerpt from MEXICAN JUMPING BEAN by Pepe Romero, published by G. P. Putnam's Sons, reprint by permission of the author. Copyright 1953 by Pepe Romero.

Excerpt from TACTICAL EXERCISE by Evelyn Waugh, reprinted by permission of Little, Brown and Company. Copyright 1954, by Evelyn Waugh.

Library of Congress Cataloging in Publication Data

Smith, Harry Allen, 1907—1976
    Don't get perconel with a chicken.

    Reprint of the ed. published by Little, Brown, Boston.
    1. Children—Anecdotes and sayings.   I. Title.
[PN6328.C5S48   1977]   818'.5'207   77-23991
ISBN 0-8128-2363-X
ISBN 0-8128-2362-1 pbk.

A FEW YEARS AGO the American newspapers made a considerable fuss over an eight-year-old French girl named Minou Drouet, a writer of poetry. She was admitted to membership in the French Society of Authors, Composers and Music Publishers on the strength of a poem which she put together in thirty minutes.

When this child's writings were first called to the attention of the Society's officers, they grew cagey and suspicious, because the French people have sharp eyes for the rogue, the fraud, and, even worse, the ghost-writer. Minou had written, for example, "Little girls' bottoms are really a wonderful gift from heaven for calming the nerves of mothers. I know perfectly well that's what they were invented for, because hands have hollows and bottoms have humps."

The Society simply refused to believe that a girl of eight would ever sit down and compose such a salute to bottoms. So Minou was challenged; and then, under supervision, she was put to work on a poem. If it

[3]

turned out to be good, she would gain membership in the Society. If bad, she would be exposed. The poem she wrote was quite literary, being concerned with feelings of heaviness and tufts of blood-colored grass and a description of herself walking on her head. It was a trifle transcendental, difficult to understand, perhaps even existentialist. My own feeling, when I read it, was that Minou actually *had* walked on her head, and hurt it.

I don't mean to be chauvinistic, but I'm prepared to argue that here in the United States we have whole legions of little children who can write rings around Minou Drouet. Our own children, when they take lead pencil in hand, are seldom abstruse. They hit hard and their meaning is usually clear. Mark Twain once said that the most useful and interesting letters are from children seven or eight years old, for "they tell all they know, and then stop." And Oliver Wendell Holmes wrote: "Pretty much all the honest truth-telling there is in the world is done by children." Both men, I feel sure, were thinking about children in their own land.

Truth-telling and complete candor and awful sincerity are to be found in both the talk and the scribblings of our small fry. A teacher asked a ten-year-old to spell the word "straight." The child spelled it correctly and then the teacher said, "Now, what does it mean?" And the child answered, "Without ginger ale."

There is also the story of a small boy who was a dinner guest at the home of a girl friend. The two youngsters bickered over who would say grace, and finally the girl's mother suggested that they *both* do the job. So the little boy started off, "In the name of the Father, and of the Son and of the Holy Ghost, Amen." And the girl, her head bowed, added with great reverence, ". . . And to the republic for which it stands."

During the last few years I have been casually collecting the literary works of children and I have noticed that while we have our share of juvenile poets, our kids seem to excel in the production of prose, whether it be the formal essay written in school, the letter from summer camp or the note left on the kitchen table for Mom. And I have always been impressed by the rugged individuality of each author, especially in the matter of spelling. My own daughter was halfway through college before I succeeded in breaking her of the habit of writing the abbreviation of *et cetera* as "ect." I have learned that it is a common error among the scribbling kids. And there are others. They write "are" when they mean "our," as in the case of Mona Espy's perceptive essay on her family's pets. They write "threw" instead of "through" and "since" instead of "sense." A surprising number of them refer to the condition of being an adult as "adultery" or "adulty." They have trouble, for some strange reason, with the spelling of "behavior," as well as "knock," and none of them ever agrees with Webster on the word "business."

I have at hand an essay which illustrates how originality can be practiced with both "knock" and "business." It is a creative work with strong moralistic overtones, written by a nine-year-old boy named Mike Peters of Reidsville, North Carolina. It was sent to me by Mike's teacher, Miss Sue Moore, and follows:

A MAN WITH A BIG NOSE
Once upon a time there lived a man. And he had a big nose. He was always stiking it into other peoples binsites. One time he stuck his nose in to a gints bin-sites. the gint said if he did not get out of his land he would knong the big nose of of his face. And he would have a little nose. One day the man went back to the gints castel the gint nocket his nose so little that you gould not see it. So that teaches you a lassen not to stick your nose into other peples binses.
the END

It is entirely possible that there are a few mistakes in spelling in the above essay; if so, Mike Peters need not feel embarrassed about it. At about the same time he was writing it, a survey was being conducted at Ohio State University. Two doctors combed through a pile of reports handed in by university students, and discovered that many of the undergraduates are atrocious spellers. The report made by the doctors contained some of the actual misspellings of the students, and included these paragraphs:

Students have reported in their medical histories such childhood illnesses as measels, bronicle nomonia, hooping cough, rumatic feavor and diptherie. During their adolescence many are afflicted with asma, accute apendisidus, heart mummers due to rhuemantic fever, stummach truble and toncilitas.

As a hobby some list swiming and bolling, some build modle airplanse, while others are interested in antigue cars and saling boats. One just enjoys listening to musik.

Many students in describing their present health will indicate it is exselent, some describe it as vary good and others simply state that they are in good phiscul and mentle condition.

The results of earlier researches into children's writings were published in *Good Housekeeping* as well as in a book which had a wide circulation. Consequently, people all over the country — and, indeed, in foreign lands — have been sending me additional examples.

[7]

Mrs. Thomas Lawton of Orlando, Florida, who would seem to be a teacher, forwarded a remarkable essay by a girl who signed her paper "Sally." It follows:

HEALTH
1. When you don't feel well you hump your back.
2. When you hump your back your intestins will be pushed together in others words squished.

If that's all there is to health, I intend to be mighty healthy from now on; at my age I have no difficulty at all humping my back. In fact, quite frequently it humps itself.

During moments of giddiness I sometimes think that the writing of history should be taken out of the hands of adult historians and turned over to the very young. An Episcopal vicar in Nevada tells me that when he was a teacher of ancient history in Providence, Rhode Island, he gave his class of youngsters an assignment to write on "The Roman Baths." One of the boys concluded his essay with:

> Sometimes the women would bath in milk and the men would hang around the baths for days.

And the whole history of the world was summed up in a few lines by a six-year-old pupil on Long Island.

His definitive work, sent me by his teacher, Mrs. Ellen Tunkel, follows:

First there was just this Adam and Eve and they had only one state. Then this Columbus sailed in his three ships and found more states. Then Davy Crocket came along and took over.

Mathematical formulae, which are always a source of great confusion to me, never seem to bother the kids. One of them wrote: "Parallel lines are lines that never meet until they run together." Another: "A circle is a round straight line with a hole in the middle." And still a third: "Things which are equal to each other are equal to anything else." These quick and easy solutions remind me of a fairly famous essay on safety composed by a New York City boy. The teacher ordered the class to write on "Means of Saving Life." (I think she had in mind such matters as artificial respiration and tourniquets and that sort of thing.) One boy turned in the following:

MEANS OF SAVING LIFE
Pins are a means of saving life by not swallowing them.

Dickie Buttenheim is a compassionate and understanding human being; at least he was all of that when he attended the second grade at Halsted School in Yonkers, New York. During his summer vacation he had visited a farm and he had become interested in pigs, or at least in the plight of pigs. He returned to school full of indignation over the fact that so many people look upon pigs as being dirty. He believed passionately that it was no fault of the pigs. He resolved to defend the good name of swine and he wrote an essay on the subject. All pigs should be grateful. The essay follows exactly as it appeared in the pages of the school paper, the *Halsted Herald*:

PIGS CAN BE CLEAN
Dickie Buttenheim Roat This Book

Pigs can be clean if you want them to. Give them a chance. If you give them a clean pen and green grass and spray them off each day they will be clean.

I saw some pigs at a farm. They were dirty. The men were feding them. They threw the mush into the troth and the mush sloped all over the ground.

And the next day the ground was muddy. Pigs would not be happy if they could not roll in the mud.

Joust make ann electric wire fenc. Then jost have a gate with electric wire. Then have a pasage way with electric wire down to the mud pile. Then when they come back from the mud pile get them in line up the pasage way. Then spray them one by one. Then when one of the pigs is sprayed, open the gate and let him go into the pen.

Don't feed pigs mush. Feed them corn. One little

baby pig at the farm, fell in the mush. But if you feed them corn they will not fell in.

They have another troth for water. Make the water clean. That is a good way to get them fat. — The end.

(By the time I got this pig essay into print, Dickie's sister, Judy, had become seven years old — Dickie's age when he composed it. She read it and snorted with sisterly indignation, declaring to her mother that Dickie had misspelled the word "roat." Her mother suggested that Judy correct it, and she did, with a flourish, making it "roate.")

The Buttenheims appear to be a literary family. More recently Dickie's sister Debbie, age ten, was given a punishment. When her parents returned home they found that Debbie had been misbehaving during their absence. She was ordered to go to her room and write a composition on "Responsibility." The result follows:

RESPONSIBILITY

Responsibility means that you are able to conduct yourself in an orderly maner without someone there ready to hit you on the head with a club. And you are trusted to be alone without getting in troble. and if you do you will tell the truth.

There is something about the sudden displacement of a child from home to summer camp that brings out remarkable literary talent. Mrs. Ruth M. Dirgo of Omaha has preserved the following letter:

> Dear Mother: Tonight the moon is shining. The wind is not blowing but when it does you can hear it in the trees. Mr. S—— said to write a letter and make it interesting and you are to write back that it is. Your son, Earl.

A guest at Grossinger's in the Catskills received the following message from her offspring at camp:

> Dear Mommy:
> Please bring some food when you come to visit me. All we get here is breakfast, dinner and supper.

Wendell Margrave has seen a postal card sent by a twelve-year-old girl from camp, which said:

> Dear mom: 3 of the girls in my tent have the dire rear.

Rosalind Russell's son once sent his famous mother a picture of himself holding an eight-foot python. The picture was inscribed:

> Dear Mom, This is my favorite snake. Love.
>   Lance

The R. W. Vespermans of Eau Claire, Wisconsin, have long cherished a letter written home by their son when he was twelve. It went:

Dear Dad,
    Please write often even if it is only a couple of dollars. Love.

                                                    Johnny

Ed Schultz of Schenectady, New York, informs me that when his brother was a child he wrote home from camp:

    Dear Mom, Vacation is all most over. See you soon, your love child,

                                                    Charles

A prominent magazine editor in New York has forwarded a camp letter written by his daughter when she was eight. It is a most provocative document, and a little tragic:

    I passed the swimming test It was easy I haven't gone to the bathroom for two days and I can't get the Kondremul bottle open Please write me to tell me what to do Love Susie.

Mrs. Kenneth B. Clarke of Brooklyn tells me that when her son went away to camp, at the age of eight, he was given a stack of postcards, already stamped and addressed, and told to write home at least once a week.
    His first card read:

    Today I rode Somky the hores.

The Clarkes made inquiry of the camp counselors, and found out what they had suspected: that their boy was riding a horse named Smokey. For the duration of his stay at camp all his messages home had to do with Somky the hores. Somky the hores ran away, or Somky the hores had a sicknes, or Somky the hores jumped over some bushs. When at last the Clarkes drove to the camp to fetch their boy home, he insisted upon introducing them to his favorite mount. He took them to the stable where they found, above the animal's stall, a sign clearly identifying him as "Somky the Hores." It had been placed there by the counselors.

The *New Yorker* seems to have reduced its acreage of camp letters during the last couple of years, but those that do appear in its pages are first rate. Here is one from a nine-year-old girl to her parents:

> Everybody in our cabin is homesick including a girl whose father and mother work here. And *they* are homesick too.

One from a twelve-year-old, soon after his arrival for his first experience in summer camp:

> Dear Mother:
>   You gave me no money because the camp said we didn't need money. But we do need money. I am happy here.
>
>   Love,
>   Jimmie
>
> P. S. Could you send me a deck of cards?

The *New Yorker*, however, has not neglected the junior authors and letter writers. The following five items are from the magazine.

A nine-year-old boy who accompanied his class to a farm in the Berkshires for a week wrote home:

> I'm safe at Otis. We started to build a tomb. I'll explain later. Good-bye.
>
> Your loving son,
> Nick

A three-and-a-half-year-old boy of Washington, Connecticut, dictated the following story:

> Once there was a little boy and he didn't like his mother; he hated his mother, because she was old and ugly. Two witches came and chopped his mother up in pieces and killed her, and threw her in the river. The little boy's father came and pulled her out, and suddenly she was young and beautiful, and the little boy still didn't like her.

A small girl in Alexandria, Virginia, whose mother had gone to a dinner party, left the following note for her on the hall table:

> Dear Mother:
> I would like you to explain about the universe when you have more time to.
>
> Love,
> Sandra

In a household where psychology was freely discussed, an eleven-year-old girl and her younger brother were packed off to bed for making too much noise. Just before retiring the daughter handed her mother this holograph:

> Dear Mother:
> I think it's about time you made an apology to me and Earl. Imagine putting us in bed at 8:45! Being mean will get you no where, being mean to others when you're mean at yourself is noway to solve a problem. I'd like to help you if you'd only let me.

A procedure for the observance of Halloween was set down in the following document, written by a nine-year-old girl for the instruction of her friend:

> Anne:
> 1. Hide behind big green sofa.
> 2. As I go like this with my horn (do do) you start in with yours like this (whooo). Make it ghostly.
> 3. When I give a long last blow ending like this (whooo do do) we start to crawl out. As they enter the door we prance upon them.
> 4. I will show you how to prance upon them before hand.
>
> Patricia

A boy in a Des Moines school is the author of a remarkable essay which, in three brief lines, contains a superb declaration of love, a brilliant demonstration of logic, and a lesson in diplomacy. The essay was sent to me by Anne Hollenbeck, who teaches in Des Moines, and follows:

> My favorite teacher is Miss Moore. Miss Moore is like a short haired dog. A dog is smart. A dog is mans best friend. I am a man.

In Chappaqua, New York, the editor of the weekly *Sun* recently sent a nine-year-old girl to the town police station with instructions to examine the blotter and write out all the mighty occurrences of the last few days. The result, which I consider to be a masterpiece of contemporary journalism, follows:

> First Mrs. Riesenkonig said she had a red setter puppy, and it turned out to belong to Mrs. Amadon. Mrs. Metcalf lost her brindle beagle, it was a female, and it was brown and white with black spots, she lost it the same day. And Mrs. Chaikin found a beagle hound and it belonged to Mrs. Riesenkonig, but it was a different Mrs. Riesenkonig. Peter Ebel had a black scotch terrier for a few days and it didn't belong to him and Mrs. Meyer lost a Kerry blue thats a dog too and they found it at Mrs. Shannahans and Mrs. Stern lost a police dog,

a small female one she said it was, and all this happened in two days. The next day Mrs. Rice heard an awful sound that sounded like a dog crying hard and they found it was a dog and it was stuck in a barb wire fence but a boy named Woodward unstuck it so it didnt cry any more I guess. That was the same day Mrs. Joy found a raccoon on her porch, and they told Mr. See about it because he lost one last week. That is all for that day. Mrs. Campbell had a gray angora cat that went out at night and didnt come back but she hopes she will find it I guess. The last thing that happened was Mr. Cunningham lost his red setter, and so did Mr. Amadon, that's funny, didnt we have him before.

Grace Kelly, now a princess, had literary ambitions when she was a child. It is recorded that at the age of fourteen she composed the following profound quatrain:

> I hate to see the sun go down
> And squeeze itself into the ground,
> Since some warm night it might get stuck
> And in the morning not get up.

Mrs. A. T. Finney of Cassville, Wisconsin, tells me of the time her fifth-graders were put to work writing an original drama. They chose their own theme: *The*

Wild West. Mrs. Finney remembers best that part of the script which read:

> The villain is caught by the poss. He is dragged before the judge.
>
> "He was caught with the goods. Caught with the brandin' iron in his hand, brandin' stolen calves. Lets string him up."
>
> "No said the judge, Justice prevails here. Give him the electric chair for life."

Mrs. Finney also recalls the case of the little girl who was told, years ago, to write on "A Vacation Adventure." Her narrative was concerned with a harrowing family expedition in a buggy, during which a cloudburst sent an avalanche of water and rocks across the roadway. The little girl's uncle was driving and brought the family through safely by his expert handling of the horses. Nevertheless, the child's account of the adventure ended with:

> Its a good thing my uncle wasnt drunk that day too or we would all have been drownd.

Mrs. Calvin A. Hyde of Durango, Colorado, was working in the kitchen one day recently when her four-year-old son, Robby, came in and announced that he had a book to write. "You write it down and I'll tell it," he said; she did, and here it is:

Once upon a time there was God up in Heaven. And God was very busy making a man. When the man was all made he said to God, "God, you're a sweet person and I like you. So when I get down to earth I'm going to be a good boy and send you back some bubble gum."

When Lila La Munyon was a little girl, she often heard arguments within the family circle over one member who seemed to be addicted to gambling. For some reason, Lila decided that poetry might effect a cure. She composed the following:

You shouldent play porker
　　And shouldent gamble
Or youll be like
　　Two eggs in a sacarmble.

Lila tells me that she placed the poem on the offending party's bed, but that it failed to reform him. It has, nevertheless, furnished much laughter in the family down through the years.

A schoolteacher in St. Louis once told her sixth-grade youngsters to write "about something you have in your homes." She has saved one entry, the work of a small boy — whose name, of course, she refuses to reveal. His essay:

DERT
In the home there is dert. It is not good to be there. And all ways should be swep up.

The late James Street's granddaughter, Rickey, began to show literary talent at an early age. She wrote her own biography of the novelist as follows:

ABOUT MY GRANDFATHER
My grandfather was important. He was famous His name was James Street. He wrote an interesting book called Good by my Lady. In the afternoon he gets his secratrie. In the evening he usually works on the book.

Apparently the rigorous life of an author, as described in that biography, didn't impress Rickey too much, for she immediately decided to try her own hand at a novel. The result:

ABOUT A GOOD MAN
Once upon a time a man who was a very important man asked his wife to make potatoes and vegetables so she did. She put in eggs and salt and other odd things. He had tea to drink. He had fruit for desert. He liked toast with butter on it so he got it. They had a very

good stove. He had a very lovely kitchen. His wife was a good cook. She liked rich food. It cost a little.

THE END

Mrs. Penelope Jarrell Fitch has resurrected an item from her girlhood, a list of rules governing the organization which she served as secretary. This is the way it goes:

GAY NIGHTIES HOBBY CLUB

Rules
(1) You may not have over three hobbys.
(2) You must not talk out of turn.
(3) Do not play the victrola to much.
(4) Do not play dolls during the meatin.
(5) Do not toch other peoples hobbys.

Fledgling authors seem to be at their very best when they are writing about animals. We have, for example, the case of Bobby Humphreys, nine. Bobby didn't make the grade with the Oakland *Tribune* last year. His older sister had been writing stories and drawing pictures and having them published in the *Tribune*, and it may be that Bobby grew envious. At any rate he sat down and composed a story and was about to send it to the newspaper when his parents got hold of it.

They decided to suppress it, but Bobby's grandmother has smuggled a copy of it to me and it is herewith published for the first time:

Once upon a time there was two monkeys and they were very very sad because they wanted a baby monkey. Dr. Brow the moneky Dr. siad they could not have a baby. One day she began to get fat so she went on a diet, but she was still getting fater and fater so she went to see her Doctor. The Doctor said you are going to have a baby. She told her husband and heres what happened. hugs and kisses, thats what happened.

From a third-grade schoolroom in Joplin, Missouri, comes a manuscript that has elements of brilliance:

THE WOLLF
The wollf kills sheep and small cows. They are related to the dog but not leshley. They do not eat vegatables. There are no wollfs in So. America. They are gray. They go to gether and kill antelops. By biteing there necks. No wollfs in Ierland.

The teacher who sent me that remarkable dissertation told me that she was slightly confused by the word "leshley." She asked the boy author what it meant. He looked at it a long time and then said: "It meant something good when I first wrote it but now I can't remember."

Fred Beck reports from California that Mrs. Harold Richardson of Whittier came home from a shopping trip to find a note written by her eight-year-old son, Harold. It said:

Dear Mom,
 When you were gone our cat came all a part in the garidge.

Love,
Harold

Mrs. Richardson, to be sure, hurried out to the garidge to see about the cat that had come all a part. It was there all right — with a new litter of kittens.

A boy attending the Bret Harte school in Chicago was looking in the front part of an encyclopedia when he came upon a message from the editors, who said that if any reader had a question that was not answered in the encyclopedia, they would be happy to answer it by mail. Well, that boy had a question for them and he wrote it out and sent it to them, as follows:

What would the swithch man do if he had swithed trains on the same track opisite each other at full speed and the swith was jamed?

I have no record of what the encyclopedia editors said in response. Probably swithched the subject.

Mrs. John Downes of Chicago has sent me a historical work which some people, I'm sure, would like to see preserved under glass in the Library of Congress. The faded manuscript, done in pencil, was the work of Mrs. Downes's sister, Jean Anderson, and was written sixty-odd years ago when the author was eight years old. Here it is:

A HISTORY OF AMERICA

I hate England because it is so proud. My dear America will not be betten by old England. I wish England was the littliest town in the world.

America fout for their country, and England did not no what they were fighting about.

How I love America because it is so smart.

I do not think the Englands would feel proud they ought to feel ashamed of their selfs.

We will wip the Englands all to peases and I have no dought that the Americans will beet the Engel.

How glad I am to be an American child. I do not care if we have not a king and queen, because I know all of us would rather be smart than have a queen and king.

THE END

Soon after it was written, long years ago, this manuscript fell into the hands of Dr. Frank Otis Ballard of Hanover College, a friend of the author's family, and Dr. Ballard composed a lengthy critique. Among other things he wrote:

Then, too, I love it for this — that the reader is not left an instant in doubt of the real point of view or attitude of the author of the History. There is nothing veiled or ambiguous, nothing evasive or oblique about it. It is a powerful discharge of sentiment, emitting dazzling light and power almost stunning.

Dr. Ballard found only one "error of fact," and that in Paragraph 2, where it says "England did not no what they were fighting about." The college president comments that "all the world knew, including the King and Cornwallis, the parliament and the people, that the English knew they were fighting about eight years."

Some jokes go back a long way.

Two small Connecticut girls named Bunny and Hallie, next-door neighbors, are wild about horses. Recently Bunny went on a trip with her family, driving through the South, and wrote back to her friend:

Dear Hallie:

If I am not home feed my bird Friday & Sunday. I have a present for you. I almost saw 2 Arabian Horses at 2 plantations we visited. See you soon. Love,

Bun

An account of a surgical operation which he saw on television was written by a ten-year-old boy, as a school composition. It was picked up by *Television Quarterly*, and then republished by John Crosby.

The boy wrote:

> About a week ago a little girl from Clevelon was operated on. She was five years old. The case was a very unusual one because the girl was born with a hole in her heart. Since the hole was just in between the left and right side, the blood ran into each other. So they had to operate. They made the operation by freezing the heart to a temperature of about 40 or 50 degrees. You see, by freezing the heart it slowed the sirculation of the heart and also slowed up the heart, so when they operated they had more time doing it. After they soed up the hole, they defrosted the girl and she was perfectly fine.

This little essay was published by the magazine to illustrate the fact that children do learn from television — the boy's spelling and sentence structure may have been slightly off-center, but he had his facts straight.

Here is another letter from camp which informs Mom and Dad that . . .

> We had a hike to Big Pond. A man came at us with a big pitch fork. It was scary. It rained all night. I lost my knapsack. A bee bit Joey. The head counselor gave him mud.

A lady member of one of Charleston's oldest and most aristocratic families has sent me an item, along with orders that her name is not to be mentioned on pain of hoss-whupping, suh. It is the work of a seven-year-old boy, dates back fifty years, and has long been cherished in the aforementioned aristocratic family. This child got fed up with the eternal admonitions to be polite toward all females. So he sat down and wrote:

> Once there was a little girl and when ever a gentel-man came into the room she got up and gave him her char and every day she sent a box of candy to every gentelman she new. She was very bullite.

Pepe Romero is the top English-language columnist in Mexico City. Some years ago Pepe made the acquaintance of an undersized Mexican boy named Henry, a peddler of lottery tickets. Henry turned out to be a lad of driving ambition, so Pepe got him a job as a page boy at the Hotel Reforma where the requirement is that a page boy must be smaller than a jockey and cute. This Henry spent much of his spare time studying English, so one day Pepe asked the boy to write a guest column for publication in the *News*. The result follows:

My name is Henry and working as page boy. I have a long time and very good practice on this so I think I will tell you, how a page boy has to give the sevice to a good or bad hotel.

The first idea that I have of the page boy is: that he must know English, not the perfect English but he just have to know the necessary for having the best attention to the tourist special in ladies, not forgeting men.

When I start in hotels I was just 11 years old now I am 14 and there is the reason that I think I can tell you something about it, hoping that this will be interesting for you.

I start in the Reforma Hotel and there I meet many people that I steel remember them all. Miss Regina Davis, Miss Helen Rosen, Mr. and Mrs. Gallagher, Mr. Lippman, that I steel meet him in the Del Prado Hotel that is my new work and here I am alreadily known for many people from the United States. As all people know when you are a boy you never get in love, but I did. I get in love with Kaye Jonassen, she was a beautiful woman and I did love her, but know I don't feel very good because she is gone to the States, but lets forget about it because I must be able to do my work every day.

Working now in the Del Prado Hotel now I know more friends, as, Mr. and Mrs. Nelson, Miss Kelly, Miss Miller, Mr. Anthony Quinn, Mr. Sam Houston, Mr. Roma, Mr. Tyrone Power and his wife Linda Christain, Mr. Rabb, Mr. Shenkel, Mr. Jones, Mr. Johnson and Mr. Clark Clark.

My ambitions are to be manager of the Hotel Del Prado, because when I be the manager the hotel is going to have a perfect order in service, attention, and a very good personal because the personal is one of the most important things in hotels.

Before I get in the Reforma Hotel I start selling lottery tickets, I was ten years, I did get good money on that but always my ambitions were to be a page boy so I start trying to be a page boy so I learn more English talk with people practice and for all the ways hoping and selling more and more in lottery tickets you have many things to do you have to give ideas to the person who ask you, Which ticket do you think is going to win the big prize? and then you give your idea and sometimes they buy and sometimes they don't but some day the manager call and he tell me, Henry I have work for you, and I ask, Which work sir, he say, Your going to work as page boy. You cant imagine how happy did I feel from that time I have telling you all about and now I tell you about my friend another page boy Eloy Olguin, which is a very good boy because he has make it very good too.

This book is a sequel to an earlier volume called *Write Me a Poem, Baby*. When the earlier book was issued, the publishers happened to think about young Jay Egan of Woonsocket, editor of a juvenile newspaper called *The Gazette*. A copy of the book was sent to Editor Egan, with a request for criticism. He wrote:

I read the book "Write Me a Poem Baby" by Mr. H. Allen Smith. I first picked up the book, I sat down near where my mother was ironing, and I started, right on the first page, laughing out loud. My mother got cureious and she started to read it and she forgot her ironing and kept on reading.

As you know, on Friday night all the good TV programs are on, well naturally I turned on the TV on and left it on. I said to myself well while I'm alone I miteas well read the book. I didnt even look at the TV that's the truth because it was much funnier than the TV. Many frazes were very funny, some were riots, andsome were not funny but a little bit interesting.

CRITICIZMS

Some of the words were too big like tentative or documents, etc. But no matter what criticizims I have I still think it is a dandy book. Sincerely yours.

Jay A. Egan

P. S. I think this is a dandy book but I don't think it will sell as good as Edwin O'Connors book "The Last Hurrah."

Written by me.

Now, it seems to me that two important things are to be learned from Jay Egan's critique. First, and most important, if you didn't read *Write Me a Poem, Baby*, now you know what you missed — a dandy book, with big words and with many funny frazes. Second, there is a lesson here for grown-up book reviewers — they should tell about the circumstances surrounding their actual reading of a book. Gilbert Highet and John K. Hutchins and Orville Prescott — those guys would never have the courtesy to inform the reader that they began by picking the book up; if they read a book while *their* mothers were ironing, they should say so, for an ironing mother in the background can have a very important effect on criticism.

P. S. Jay Egan hit it right on the nose — that dandy book sold real good but not as good as *The Last Hurrah*.

Earl Wilson once published a composition written by a ten-year-old Long Island boy, an only child. It said, somewhat mysteriously:

A BROTHER
I wouldn't mind having a brother. But the trouble is I dont. And I won't because the person who does it cant do it.

Several years ago a boy named Robert Hanson Stiver wrote a school composition which started out as an adventure story. In the middle of it, however, there was a sudden change of mood, and Robert revealed himself as a person grown skeptical about radio and television commercials. In his story he used real trade names, but I don't have his courage and have substituted blanks. Here is the story:

AN EXCITING EXPERIENCE

One Winter night my brothers and I went fishing off an old bridge. All of a sudden a board gave way and my big brother went in the river. None of us could swim, so I took out my flashlight with new —— batteries and a bulb, and started signaling. After about two minutes it went out. My younger brother had a flashlight with —— batteries and a bulb, and I started signaling with it. After about two hours some men went in the river and pulled my brother out. The flashlight was still burning brightly.

After this don't believe all you hear about —— batteries. They don't have any more nine lives than I do.

Rudolph Elie, late columnist for the Boston *Herald*, kept abreast of juvenile writing in his area. Once he reported on a new newspaper called *Aircraft*, put out by two boys, Dave Clinkman and Geoff Tupper in Marblehead. Editor Tupper is author of a serial story entitled "The Surprise Attack" in which Ivan, one of the heroes, has discovered that the people of Venus breathe cobalt. Columnist Elie also noted a brilliant editorial in *Aircraft*, inspired by a fatal accident in Marblehead. The editorial:

What do you get by careless driving? In the end, practically nothing.

Mrs. J. Hoyt Geer of Dallas has furnished me with some of the literary works of her daughter, Genie. Among Genie's essays, all of which were written at the age of seven, is one which manages to compress the mystery of life into one Hemingwayish sentence:

A COW
In the medo there was a larg cow. It had a baby. The baby was small. It ate the gras and it was a good cow. And it had a baby and it had a baby and on it went.

Here are three more essays by Genie:

THE BAND
A band came to twon and there was a trumpit a banjo a piano and all sorts off things a clown that was so funny it made evreine laugh. The band played beautiful music. And some off the songs were a sunny day. a rainbow. and love. And they made lots off money all there lives.

(Sounds like Lawrence Welk.)

TWO MICE AND ONE CAT
There was to mice and one cat. Now . . . the cat liked to chase the mice. but the mice all-wase tricked him. But one day he ate them up. Oh! a unarmas anuml came and ate him up. Oh! and that was the end.

THE RITER

One day a riter came to town and started makeing books and evreone bought them. But one day he went broke. And that was the end and seemed to him it was a bad day. But evre once in a while he'd be lucky. But that was all THE END.

(This little girl *knows* about things!)

Genie Geer arrived at the age of eight, and wrote the following newsy letter to her grandmother:

Dear Nannie

I am now sick with a cold, yet I can get around. I don't have any fever, I had grapefruit, and apple juice, and castoria of course! Christmas is getting near. I'v had a lot of fun in school and have been learning to borrow in sabtrack-shoin. Well, about Three nights befor Dec. 3 Mom thought that she heard rain, and looked out of the den door, she saw a long pink tail in the garbage (it was tipped over) and the thing with the pink tail backed out, it was at least 12½ feet long! and Mom screamed it was a *oppossom!* Daddy said that it would make mintsmeat out of the Cat! but I was glad it didn't. Thats all I can thing of but pretty soon I will wright another letter.

Lots of love x x x x x

Genie

Tess Crager's daughter, Gretchen, is now married to a Yale professor; but when she was ten years old,

[35]

way down yonder in New Orleans, she composed what to me is one of the greatest of all poems concerning that glorious season when the sap rises. The poem was sent to me by Mary Rose Bradford:

SPRING
The goat meets the goat,
The ram meets the ram,
I will go fowit
And meet my man.

Mrs. Lucie Read of Salem, Massachusetts, remembers a poem written by a young friend of hers many years ago. The title of the poem was "The Dead Child." The first part told of how the narrator went into "a dark shamber" where she saw the dead child. The concluding lines were:

Its soul was taken by the Lord
And there it lay as stiff as a board.
It might have been my dearest joy,
Was it a girl, or was it a boy?

Tom Bissell is still editing his mimeographed newspaper, *The Fenelon Place Journal*, over in Connecticut. Tom is the son of Richard Bissell, the author and playwright, who is always referred to in the *Journal* as "The Famous Author." The following item appeared in the BIG HOLIDAY ISSUE!!! of the *Journal*:

[36]

WHAT I GOT FOR CHRISTMAS
by Sam Bissell, age 6
(*A Special Interview*)

When I woke up I came downstairs and saw a Christmas stocking full of candy and presents, and I had a apple and a tangerine and also I had a lot of stuff. Then I went back upstairs again. Also I took everything out of my stocking and then I got dressed. I went downstairs and I had breakfast and then Papa said we should stay in line and then Papa came back and waved his hand and we walked in the Christmas room, and everybody saw their Christmas presents and also a big pretty Christmas tree that Santa brought. Then we opened our Christmas prenesces and also I got ummm a drum and a cement truck from Santa Claus. I got a west guitar from Roy Rogers and Santa Claus. It's brown. I ate up all of my candy and Aunt Bess and Aunt Marguerite gave it to me. And Aunt Susan and Uncle Fred gave me some games of cards, Forest Friends, and also I got a engineer game. And Sis gave me a neat shirt. Then we opened the pool game. Then all the presents were opened so we ate lunch. [At this point the editor reread the story to Sam which Sam had just dictated to him. Sam continued] I goofed. Grandma and Grandpa really gave me those games. Aunt Susan and Uncle Fred gave me that gun holster and gun and that big brown thing. [A jug, ED.]

Debby Choate, who lives on Riverside Drive in New York, reports to me that she once had a teacher named

[37]

Michael So-and-so whom she disliked intensely, so she wrote a poem about him:

EPITAP

Here lies Black Mike
Never to be forgot,
We've put a flower at his head,
At t'other end — a pot.

A teacher in St. Michael's School at Hoban Heights, Pennsylvania, collected a few "boners" she found in papers turned in by her pupils. These were printed in a diocese newspaper, then picked up by Robert Sylvester of the New York *News*, and now it's my turn:

We dont raise silk worms in the U. S. because the U. S. gets her silk from rayon. He is a much larger animal and gives more silk.

Denver is just below the "O" in Colorado.

An adjective is a word hanging down from a noun.

They don't raise anything in Kansas but alpaca grain and they have to irritate that to make it grow.

The Mediterranean and the Red Sea are connected by the sewage canal.

Marconi invented the Atlantic ocean.

Abraham Lincoln was shot by Clare Boothe Luce.

When a man has more than one wife he is a pigamist.

[38]

An epidemic is a needle that puts you to sleep.

A spinster is a bachelors wife.

Chicago is nearly at the bottom of Lake Michigan.

The equator is a menagerie lion running around the earth and through Africa.

The sun never sets on the British Empire because it is in the East and the sun sets in the West.

Minute Men were called that because they stopped to get ready a minute.

When you breath you inspire and when you don't you expire.

A blizzard is the inside of a fowl.

Another item of this type, written by a second-grader:

The minus sign means take away. The plus sign means give it back.

Marc Antony Russell, son of a Chicago magazine editor, was six years old when he decided the time had come for him to begin writing plays. Though an accomplished dramatist, Marc was no good at penmanship, so he dictated his first play to his mother. "It was taken down verbatim," reports his father. "He dictated the title first, then the cast, and so on. He also made very sure of stage directions and was insistent about the use of parentheses." Here is Marc's drama:

THE BIBLE BUSTED

Cast

Television reader
Television interrupter
Policeman
Society lady

Scene

A television station.

TV READER: The Lord said unto my Lord, sit thou at my right hand, until I make thine enemies thy footstool. Thy . . .

TV INTERRUPTER: What ya doin' there son?

TV READER: Will you please get out of the television studio and stop interrupting?

TV INTERRUPTER: No I will not get out.

TV READER: Then I'll call the police.

TV INTERRUPTER: Eek!

TV READER: (*picking up telephone*) Send a policeman to the television studio and catch a TV interrupter.

(*A screeching sound is heard from far off*)

TV INTERRUPTER AND TV READER: I hear a screeching sound getting louder and louder.

POLICEMAN: (*calling from the ground up to the window*) Is this the place you wanted me to come to?

TV READER: Yes.

TV INTERRUPTER: Help! Get me out of here.

POLICEMAN: Ha. Ha. I've got you now.

TV READER: Look out, you're going to bust the Bible.

POLICEMAN AND TV INTERRUPTER: Eek!

TV READER: Look out!

(They crash to the floor)
TV READER: Too late, you busted it. See what you've done.
SOCIETY LADY: OOH! Oh, my!

THE END

I suspect that this Marc Antony Russell has the makings of some kind of genius in him. A few months after he wrote his first play, he went to work on a project which he called *Webster's Dictionary of Goofy Words*. The original manuscript was printed in block letters on both sides of four large shirt cardboards. One line, in large letters, said, REG. U. S. PAT. OFF. I don't have the space to include all of the words and definitions, but here are some of them:

ABASAB — A one hundred foot long blister.
BAR — A place people go when they want to get drunk.
BUMBUMSKILOPUSUS — A disease so terrible that you die.
BARD — A pen that looks like a pencil.
DOBERMAN — A person that weighs 2,030 pounds.
DARD — A person that falls out of the window every second.
EB — A frame that a baby swing could go on.
EBERCO — Exactly like an eb except for its shape.
FABBER — A person that talks all their life and never stops.
GABEO — A doorstep in Mexico.

GIZABOO — A horrible looking monster with a voice like a teddy bear.

HARDY — Somebody that bangs on the table very hard.

HAP — Half happy.

IERE — A snow more slippery than regular snow or ice.

JAZZABAR — A drunk jazz quartet.

KASABAR — An upside-down Checker Cab.

NAC — A person named Mac standing on their head.

OBEO — A piano key in Africa.

POEMKI — Translated from Polish meaning a goofy magazine.

PANNER — A painter standing on his head.

PAMMER — A photograph of dinosaurs.

QUOTO — A silly ditto mark.

RAXS — Noisy food.

SEBAR — Something to eat. Only the empire state bldg likes the taste of it.

WONSOME — The same meaning as "bard."

XIKAMOR — A baby polar bear.

As has been said before, when a child sets his mind to the task of writing a stern and forceful letter, he doesn't fool around. From Fort Collins, Colorado, comes the story of a boy who spent the entire spring selling garden seed from door to door in order to get a premium which was pictured in glorious color in the magazine ad. Here is the letter he wrote to the perfidious corporation:

Dear Sir —

You are a chiseler and a cheat. You were suppose to send a baseball glove like the one in the picture. You dident. You were supposed to send an extra prize also. You dident.

Your enemy,
Roy——

PS — Remember when I get mad I stay mad.

Mrs. Kenneth Switzer of Flagstaff, Arizona, was often amused by the way her five-year-old, Martha, would sit down and tell stories to little Ann, who was only one. Mrs. Switzer decided she'd eavesdrop and write down one of the stories as it came from Martha's lips. She was fortunate enough to be listening on the day when Martha chose to narrate the life of Jesus. This is how it went:

Once upon a time a man and a lady lived in Yoldey. They didn't have any babies, but soon God sent them a sweet little baby named Jesus. They named him Jesus. He grew and grew without sucking his thumb. When he got as big as Mike [a neighbor boy] they went up to Igley. Jesus talked to the big men. They gave him presents. He loved children and told the mothers and daddies to back up and let the children sit on his lap. Then he rode to Pondey on a little donkey. The people waved palm branches at him and called "hi" at him. When they ate supper he stood up and fussed at the men for bad manners. Don't eat food with your knife. The men began not liking him, and made him carry a heavy old wooden cross. It scratched his back and made it bleed.

The story seems to have ended there but, as it stands, it's got a lot in it. If you study it carefully you'll find that even the undertones have undertones.

Another letter from camp, courtesy of the *New York Herald Tribune*:

Dear Mom How are you I am studying Zoo-olgy. It is neat. I have 2 frogs and a lizzard. Love.

Dick

A boy named Richard Parry contributed his version of "Jack and the Beanstalk" to a school paper, the *Buckley Beagle*, in California; and Gene Sherman thought the story was so exciting that he reprinted it in his column. Here it is:

A long time ago, there wus a little boy named Jack. His mother wus very poor and his father was ded and his cow did not give milk. So his mother tolds him to go to town. By and by he met a pedler. When Jak wausent looking the pedler pulled the cow throo the booshs. When Jack turned around he found five culerd

[44]

beans on the fens. Jack started to crie becus he knew he wood get in trubl. He was rite.

When he came home his mother threw the beands away in a bad temper. Over night sumthing started to grow. Yesterday before it started to grow a stemroaler possht the beans in the growned. It grew one foot past the enisfere. He diddint know a gient so he started to clime into trubl. When he got their he saw a harp. The second time he went up he saw a hen that lade gold eggs and the third time he saw the giente. The giente dropped a bag of gold. Jack slide down the bean stalk and shook it so the gient fell and made a hole and they livd hapelly ever after.

One of these days, when I get caught up on everything, I'm going to sit down for several hours and see if I can't figure out that word "enisfere." I have a hunch it is the stuff gobbed up on the other side of the stratosphere.

In the same *Buckley Beagle* is a nature note contributed by Tom Huntington. It says:

> We have an owl tree in our yard full of holes and owls keep coming out all night.

That item has a bad effect on me, especially on sleepless nights, when a vision seems to appear before me — a tree with a lot of holes in it, and steady streams of owls pouring out of each hole. It's a frightening sort of thing because one lone and lorn owl is about all the owl I can cope with.

My own Nobel and Pulitzer awards already have been given to an assortment of Espy children on the basis of writings used in my earlier book. There are more. The following note was written by Cassy Espy, and again it must be explained that Joey and Freddy are her sisters, not her brothers. Pet is a cat.

Dear mommy:
    I love you. I love you so much that I don't no what to do. I want to tell you about a little tale about Pet and I. Pet and I went out walking we herd a sound. It went tap tap tap. It was Joey and Freddy taping on a tree. I said to Joey and Freddy I think you are little Birds. Joey and Freddy said to me I think you are a little worm.

Love,
Cassy

And we find included among the unpublished papers of Joanna Espy (Joey) the following moral dissertation:

LAUGHS, PRANKS AND SURPRISES
The Harmful Prank

After we had moved in for the first Halloween in our new neighborhood a boy was telling us about how all the other Halloweens had been like. This boy told me and my sisters that a group of boys got together and went around on a lot of streets with lots of pumpkins and climb in the trees with the pumpkins and anyone that walked under would get a pumpkin dropped on their heads. He also told that they were mean to little animals and killed them and threw them at people. They only killed mice if they could find any.

It is bad to be mean to animals just because it is halloween and it would be a disgusting sight. Someone could be hurt easily if a pumpkin was thrown at someone or on anybodys head. Halloween is for fun and so the little kids can get candy but it also can be fun for the elder children to play pranks that arent harmful.

Not long ago the Franklin Watts company, publishers of *The First Book of Bees*, received the following letter:

Dear Sir:

Pleas send me a queen bee. I want to start a bee colony. How much does it cost or does it cost anything? My daddy is goging to help me start one. If you have any instructions please send me some of them. This is my first time to have a beehive. Send me a list of the things I have to have. I will by them. (signed) Year Frend.

PS. if it coust anything dont send me the bee but how much it cost and the instructions how to do it.

In the summer of 1957 the publishing house of Doubleday & Company received a manuscript from Longview, Texas, and with it a letter which said:

I am twelve years old and this is my first attempt at a written story and it is wished that it meets with your approval. Should you desire to publish this story, please advise the writer at the above address. The name of this story should be You Dog. Yours very truly.

David L. Hill

Ann Durell of Doubleday, knowing that I have been interested in such manuscripts, sent David's along to me and I take great pleasure in publishing it here, in full:

PART I — THE RIOT

One night a riot was started among the patients, the police and staff came to stop it. It wasn't until the next morining that . . . Percy H. Barnes was missing from the Red Rock Institution for the Insane. Percy had the same night stolen a car from a used car shop and killed the owner in cold blood from a blunt instrument. The next day driving along at a medium rate of speed Percy thought that he was free as a bird.

But meanwhile in the large city of Los Angeles a police search was in full flight. Meantime Percy had stopped at a filling station late that afternoon, the service station attendant came to the car, Ethyl the man replied solomnly to the Insane man. Percy nodded politely, the man thought he had seen the man before but he didn't know where. So while Percy H. Barnes was waiting there in the car the man sneaked into his office to phone the police, the man knew who he was from a wanted poster he had noticed.

PART II — THE MURDER

Percy had become suspicious at the man's ways so Percy got out of the car he had killed a man to get and walked into the office unmolested by the service station man, the man was calling the police Percy thought then he was sure of it, the man was saying, hello police headquarters?, Percy H. Barnes is in my station here on highway 204. The policeman replied 204 you said? Yes Sir, Hurry please hurry, the man slammed the receiver on the hook and turned around there stood Percy H. Barnes, no please no, "arrrgggghhh" Percy had strangled the man to death.

PART III — THE CHASE

Hello, Hello, click, click, click went the receiver but there was no answer to the policemans frantic attempts to make contact with the man. Both men Percy Barnes had murdered were elderly. Percy thought as he was making his escape, Hmmm it seems to me I remember a bridge in this part of the country, I think its the highest one in the world, I've forgotten the name of it but they would never find me there, that is if nobody were there to tell them I was there, Ha Ha ha laughed Percy in wild fiendish laughteer. It was out of pure good fortune for Percy to find the bridge the very next day by asking a fellow tourist.

PART IV — 2 MURDERS ADDED

Percy stopped the car and hid it from view in the brush and weeds about a block from the bridge.

Percy Hennington Barnes last seen driving a black sedan on highway 204 said the broadcaster. Now they had a all-points alert out for Percy H. Barnes escaped patient from Red Rock Institution. A stroke of luck granted this wish for Percy H. Barnes, there had not been a tourist at the Royal Gorge bridge that day and thier wasnt one thier yet to be witness to the murder of the three men in the little house on the thousand ft. bridge.

Percy meanwhile forced the three men to get in one of the lifts to take people down in the gorge. The idea was Percy thought nobody would be as likely to see him murder the men down in the gorge. Percy then hit two of the men in the temples striking them dead instantly, he used an iron bar for the murders, he was about to strike the other man when a voice rang out from the top of the gorge. O. k. thats enough, come on Percy get in one of the lifts and come back up or do we have to come down and get you. While all this is going on the automatic Juke box puts on a record called "Talking to the Blues." Yo'll never get me you dumb Jackass flatfeet, with a wild rage of terror Percy H. Barnes tried to climb the almost sheer canyon wall. Come on down Percy, you'll never make that climb. Percy I'll give you one minute to make up your mind.

PART V — THE FATAL FALL

Percy during the minute had been wasting it trying to climb the wall. O. K. Percy your time is up, let him have it boys. Percy had just grasped a girder of the top of the bridge when the police let go with blazes of machine gun fire. Percy caught all of it in the back, dust flew out of the dirty brown leather jacket and Percy's grasp on the girder weakened and Percy finally gave way to the flying bullets, Aiiiiiiiiieeeeeee. Percy fell one thousand ft. to the canyon far below. Percys arm fell limply two seconds after he had hit bottom.

PART VI — YOU DOG

The police loaded Percy's crushed body into one of the lifts and sent him back up to the top of the bridge and put his body in the black herse and the sirens moaned very loud and then cut down low to here the last sentence of "Talking to the blues" and the word, "You Dog."

THE END

It pleasures me to report that I have received a holograph letter from David L. Hill himself, granting me permission to use "YOU DOG" in this book, and telling me that if I want them, he has two other novels finished, namely, "A STAB IN THE DARK" and "THE MADMAN STALKS THE CITY." I might add that he writes, appropriately enough, in red ink.

The manner in which some little boys occupy their time is illustrated in an essay written by Dennis Heinemann of Los Angeles and passed along to posterity by Matt Weinstock, as follows:

A little boy was looking at his fish. They werent doing anything so he went into his room and read a book. Some friends came over. They played records. Davy Crocket was their favorite. They played it 200 times and then went to bed they were so tired.

Another boy, in the same school as Dennis, was Bruce Brill and his essay demonstrates the manner in which jungle beasts occupy their time:

> Once there was a giraffe. He lived in the jungle. He liked to eat grass and bananas and leaves. At night he visited the other animals. They talked and played poker and drank lemonade until midnight.

That poker game fascinates me; I'd dearly love to see a giraffe worrying over his hole card.

The American father of today is often inclined to boast to his indolent son how hard he worked when he was a boy. In most cases he talks of a paper route, or of cutting grass. But when James H. Easley of South Bend, Indiana, reaches the point where he needs to boast of his first job, he can truthfully say, "I was in the insurance business. The *dog* insurance business."

James organized his dog insurance business when he was ten years old. He worked at it for a year or two and then abandoned it to take up a career as a writer of mystery stories. The following document, which he wrote during his first year in business, was sent to me by his aunt:

REPORT
My dear friends and agents of the company,
I don't want you to be disappointed if in this first

year we do not have enough money Because I don't figger to. We have what you might call a start on a Shoestring, inother words without any money. For that reason this year will be a tough one. If this co. insures 6 dogs and six dogs die what do you think we have? We have a broke company.

LESSON 1. ORGANIZING

To start a company you must have a lot of money. Second you must get a Liscense. Now go out and sell. The trouble is we do not have anything on this list.

LESSON 2. TWO WAYS OF SELLING

The two ways of selling are very fine. The first one is a very modern way, it is called direct mail letters. To proseed you have to write a very polite letter telling your prospects that dog insurance is just what they need give them your business address and tell them to call on you at any time. The second way is called Who's Who. The agent must know who has a dog and who has not. These are the two methods. You can use either one, but in a small town I prefer the Who's Who, it works better. In a city the direct mail is best.

THE WAY THE INSURANCE WORLD REVOLVES

The way the insurance world revolves is harder than you think. The first step is to sell a policy and then collect the premium ($1). From there on you are in danger. For example, a couple of weeks after a policy is sold the dog gets hit by a car and the hospital bill is $10.00 the company must pay that Bill. Then say two weeks later the dogs eats too much and is sick and that Bill is $5.00. The company must pay the $5.00

then he is all through because $10.00 and $5.00 is $15.00 and that is what he is insured for. Then a week later he gets the flew and the Bill is for $5.00 and the co. does not have to pay that because he has paid out to the dogs Master all that the dog was insured for so the only thing for him to do is to wait another year and buy another policy.

BEST OF LUCK

James H. Easley, Pres.

Dolly Reitz, who reitz for the Los Angeles *Mirror-News*, has a daughter called Eight, and Eight got a letter from one of her friends. On the first page it said:

I love you. I love you. I love you. I love you. I love you.

On the next page it said:

Why dont you invite me to stay at your house overnight. Someday. Now when we play we are Prince and Princess. When we grow up we will be King and Queen. We will play in the Sprinklers.

Mrs. Frank L. West of Pacific Palisades has forwarded a Christmas list typed out by her son Marshall when he was eight. It follows:

CHRISTMAS LIST

legend

\# very much needed   % probabal   & fantasy

  & L. Daizy bb Air Rifle Carbine
  % Wrist watch
  & Supply of bbs
  # Couple of eversharps 59¢ Sees Robuck
  % Pack catnip seed
  # Book on simplified atomic engry
HaHa New racer bycicle
  # Set of cleats
  & Electric motor (with dry battry)
  & Water pistol (49¢ Western Auto)
  % Lots of books
  # Money

In 1957 Virginia Meholin, nine years old, of Steubenville, Ohio, wrote a letter to her Aunt Peg. The purpose of the letter was to thank her Aunt Peg for a birthday gift, but Virginia knew that such a letter should not be abrupt, that it should be newsy. The letter found its way eventually to Aunt Peg's daughter in far-off Beirut, Lebanon, and Aunt Peg's daughter, Mrs. John Koenreich, sent it along to me.

Here it is:

Dear Aunt Peg,

    Thank you for my lovely sweater. I have really needed it. I wear it to school when it is warm enough.

    Our cat was in heat a couple of days ago and wanted to get married. She accidently got out. We could not find her so she had to stay out all night. In the morning I asked daddy if the cat was back yet. He looked out the window and said, "yes, oh golly yes!" I looked out and guess what? Miss Meow had *Two* boy friends. We let Miss Meow in and one of the cats left. The other cat started meowing. I think he was saying, "hey, beautiful come on out." Daddy got mad and chased him away. Now our cat will have babies. She will be spaded after she has them and they are older.

An eleven-year-old schoolboy in New York was given the assignment of reading two books by Mark Twain and writing a report on them. The report follows:

MARK TWAIN BOOKS

The Prince and the Pauper was about two boys that looked like. One boy was a prince and the other was a pauper.

One day the two boys came together in the palace after talking for a while the prince wanted to see how it felt being dressed like a pauper so they exchanged clothes just then one of the guards came in. When he saw the pauper he was asked to leave the palace. The pauper said he was the real prince and the prince the pauper but the guard didn't believe the boy. The guard send the real prince out of the palace.

The real prince had to beg and steal for his father. More than one thing happened to the real prince, while the pauper was having a real good time but always saying I am not the real prince. The pauper had a mean father so the father took the boy away with him even though the boy kept saying I am the prince. The father only laughed.

At the end of the real prince is belived. but he saw how mean the paupers father was so he made him his vallet and they lived together.

Huckelberry Fins is a very good book to read because it has a lot of adventure in it. Huckelberry Finn is a kid that ran away from his house because he thought that his parents did not like him. So he went away and he got lost and his parents found his bed empty and his father phone the police and they when and found him. I'm sure that any of you will enjoy this book.

I hate to be a tattletale, but if that boy's teacher wants my opinion, I think that he actually read *The Prince and the Pauper*, but I don't think he read a lick of Huck Finn, because I've read it several times and I could swear that nobody in it ever phones the police.

A boy in New Jersey turned in the following remarkable piece of literary criticism:

BOOK REPORT
The book I report is Tarzan and the ant men. Their is no report because it would tell you how it tirned out.

When she was ten Susan McClelland went from Indiana to California to spend some time with her grandmother. In her first experience with letter-writing she reported back to her mother:

I met a new girl and her name is Carloin Boson and she is 14 and lives in hillsburro. We have gone horse riding with her. Please ask Dicky if he would wright and toll him happy birthday, OK. So Tinia (dog) ses woof huh, well tell her woof right back (hellow). We have gone to San fransisco qwight a few times. I had a nice trip and I had a fruit snack and then a half an hour later we had our Big dinner. there was fried salmnon a big salid and salid dressing salt and peper suger tea and milk and a big dissert. In swimming I made Swimmer, there is a san flee, low Grop, Mino, Middel Group, and Swimner, highest Groep, and I made swinner in my first week.

Love,
Susan M.

In my fat file of children's writings I have come upon a single sheet from a school composition book, with five words printed on it in large letters. The only identification is the name Stephen Sanborn, written on the back. The five words are:

WET
PANT
YOUS
BAKE
DOOR

Of Evelyn Waugh, Charles J. Rolo has written: "There are few contemporary writers of the first rank whose imagination runs to such appalling and macabre inventions as Waugh's does; and there is none who carries audacity to such lengths . . ."

In the course of collecting material for an omnibus of Waugh's writings, Mr. Rolo discovered that the Englishman had composed his first novel at the age of seven years and one month. Here it is, complete:

THE CURSE OF THE HORSE RACE
CHAPTER I
Betting

I bet you 500 pounds I'll win. The speeker was Rupert a man of about 25 he had a dark bushy mistarsh and flashing eyes.

I shouldnot trust to much on your horse said Tom for ineed he had not the sum to spear.

The race was to take pleace at ten the following morning.

CHAPTER II
The Race

The next morning Tom took his seat in the gront stand while Rupert mounted Sally (which was his horse) with the others to wate for the pistol shot which would anounse the start.

The race was soon over and Rupet had lost. What was he to do could he do the deed? Yes I'll *kill* him in the night, he though

CHAPTER III

The Fire

Rupert crept stedfustly along with out a sound but as he drew his sword it squeeked a little this awoke Tom seasing a candle he lit it just as that moment Rupert struck and sent the candle flying

The candle lit the curtain Rupert trying to get away tumbled over the bed Tom maid a dash for the door and cleided with a perlisman who had come to see what was the matter and a panic took place.

CHAPTER IV

Explaind

While Tom and the peliesman were escaping through the door Rupert was adopting quite a diffrat methard of escape he puld the matris of the bed and hurled the it out of the window then jumed out he landed safe and sound on the matris then began to run for all he was worth

Now let us leave Rupert and turn to Tom and the peliesman as soon as they got out Tom told the peliesman what had hapened.

CHAPTER V

Hot on the Trail

"See there he is" said Tom "We must follow him and take him to prizen" said the peliesman.

Theres no time to spere said Tom letts get horses said the peliesman so they bort horses and and galerpin in the direcion thet had seen him go.

On they went until they were face to face with each other. the peliesman lept from his horse only to be

[60]

stabed to the hart by Rupert then Tom jumped down and got Rupert a smart blow on the cheak.

CHAPTER VI
A Deadly Fight

This enraged Rupert that that he shouted and made a plung but Tom was too quick for him artfully dogeing the sword he brout his sword round on Ruperts other cheak.

Just at that moment Ruper slashed killed the peliesmans horse then lept on Toms horse and golapt off.

CHAPTER VII
The Mysterious Man

Of course ther was no chance of catching him on foot so Tom walked to the nearest inn to stay the night but it was ful up he had to share with another man.

Thou Tom was yery tired he could not sleep, their was something about the man he was he did not like he reminded him of some one he didnot know who.

Sudnly he felt something moveing on the bed looking up he saw the man fully dressed just getting off the bed

CHAPTER VIII
Run to Erth

Now Tom could see that the mysteraous man was Rupert. Has he come to do a merder? Or has he only cometostay the night? thees were the thoughts that rushed throu Toms head.

he lay still to what Rupert would do first he opened a cuberd and took out a small letter bag from this he

too some thing wich made Toms blud turn cold it was
a bistol Tom lept forward and seesed Rupert by the
throught and flung him to the ground

then snaching a bit of robe from the ground he bound
Rupert hand and foot.

CHAPTER IX
Hung

then Tom drest hinself then Ton took Rupert to
the puliese cort Rupert was hung for killing the pulies-
man. I hope the story will be a leson to you never to
bet.

Thus the glorious ending of it. I admire the moral
in it and I should like to make a couple of critical ob-
servations. Young Evelyn Waugh, in common with
almost all adolescent fiction writers, has the valuable
trait of achieving intense excitement within his own
breast whenever his story grows exciting. At those moments, the young writer has no time to worry over the
niceties of either spelling or of punctuation.

There is the matter, too, of the perlisman (or peliesman) with whom Tom cleided. That clizzion was a
bad thing for the peliesman for he ended up dead (for
a long time there I thought it was only his horse that
got killed, but even the English wouldn't hang Rupert
for killing a horse). I was sorry, too, about that horse,
for when he wasn't galerpin he golapt. And I have

never in all my reading seen the word "cuberd" spelled better.

All that is actually known about the notorious Outlaw Club of Old Roaring Brook Road is contained in three short documents found by Mrs. Jane Choate in the gang's den. The Outlaw Club began in a shack built by its members but the shack was too cold for winter meetings and the club's affairs were moved indoors — into a basement storeroom in the Choate house. This is where Mrs. Choate found the aforementioned documents.

The first appears to be a sort of charter, and follows:

CLUB RULES ABOUT DEWS

WEEKS TOATAL 40¢	IF DEWS NOT
MOUNTHS TOATAL $1.60	PAYED THAT BOY
YEARS TOATAL $17.60	WILL NOT BE PROTECTED.

PS. (WE WANT MONEY FOR A TENT.)

1. NO SWERING.
2. DO WHAT YOU ARE TOLD.
3. HELP AT DESK WORK.
4. GO ON DUTY WHEN TOLD.
5. KEEP SILENT ABOUT LOCATION AND CLUB ITSELF.
6. DON'T TELL SECRETS OF CLUB.
7. DON'T GO IN CLUB WITH OUT PERMISSION.
8. DON'T TUCH DEWS.

9. DON'T BRAG ABOUT CLUB OR YOURSELF.
10. OBAY RULES OF CLUB.

NORTON (PRESIDENT)

PLATT (VICE PRESIDENT)

FRIS (SECUTARY AND GENERAL)

CHOATE (TREASUAR)

The seeds of dissension are apparent in that charter. I guessed that the document was drawn up by a dictator, who demanded subservience from his subordinates.

The second paper is a letter:

Dear John,

I am very mad because you have not ben keeping up the club meatings even if ½ the club is absent. I do not like the way you and some outher members have been telling their parents about the club actitives. we will have to move the club if you don,t be on your lookout. I think we need a new secuarty because you never send out notices about the next meating. I am sending the code with this I want it distrubtied BY MAIL. I have 100 yds. of walki-talki wire and I have one reciveing and sending instrement with one boy scout code machine. will you try to get up a meating? will you send out the notices insted of makeing me do it? (if you don,t some body else will take over.

Sincerly

yours,

Nat

PS. there is one club copy it is marked keep one for your self and send one to: taffy and eric i will keep one for myself, Keep all the letters I send you and the club copy code hidden in the club.

That one letter alone shows that trouble is brewing, that Nat is in a temper and that if conditions don't improve, some changes are going to be made. Apparently John got up a meating, and it was lovely and loud, for the next and final letter reads:

DEAR JOHN,

I THINK THAT IF WE KEEP GOING THE WAY WE ARE WE WILL GO ON THE ROCKS WE HAVE TO GET MORE SPEARET IF WE KEEP HAVEING SPATS WITH EACH OUTHER THIS CLUB WILL FALL APART

SINCEARLY,

NAT

And that's precisely what happened. They got more spearet, but it was the spearet of discontent and rebellion, and the Outlaw Club did indeed fall apart. Code and all.

The members of the Outlaw Club don't strike me as having shown much in the way of corruption and delinquency. Any time a *secret* club of boys has as its first rule NO SWERING, then you can figure its members are not going to be out stealing hub caps and slashing convertible tops and mugging citizens.

[65]

Olivia Mellan and several of her friends "put on a poem festival" on Long Island not long ago. Olivia, who was ten, and the other girls all wrote poems and made a little book to contain them. Then at the "poem festival" each girl got up and read her own compositions.

One by Olivia herself goes:

If ever you should visit my house,
　If you should hear a boom,
Have no fear. Don't worry.
　It's just from my brother's room.
If you should ever see that mess,
　You'd probably blame my mother;
But the one that takes all the blame, I guess,
　Is my naughty, little brother.
If ever you should visit us,
　You'll see this little monster;
He's cute he's smart,
He'll creep into your heart,
　But he's a booby trap kind of youngster.

Another of Olivia's poems is titled "Thinking about Professions" and would seem to indicate an end to ambition. It follows:

Thinking about professions,
　Is like difficult classroom sessions,
Wondering what you'll be when you grow up;
　Well, finally you decide,

To be a housewife and a bride,
And never win a trophy or a cup.

The author of the following poem is a girl of ten,
and it is directed at her sister, who is two or three years
older. Their mother let me copy it with the proviso
that I use no names — she wants a semblance of peace
in her family. The poem:

THAT HORRIBLE SISTER

I hate my sister,
  Oh boy and how,
I'd trade her in
  Jersey cow.
She hits me, she hurts me,
  Calls me names,
I tell mummy —
  She gets the blame.
But when my brother
  Comes home from Groton,
Then her life
  Is really rotton.
He hits her, hurts her,
  Calls her names,
But then it is a different game.
Does he get scolded —
  No not he,
For he's the boy we're glad to see.
But when he goes back,
  Woe is me
When I see her,
I run up a tree.

[67]

A second-grade teacher in Milwaukee greeted her children at the beginning of a new term with an assignment to write a composition on "something important you learned during your vacation." Among the essays turned in was the following:

WHAT I LEARND ON MY VACATTION

DONT GET PERCONEL WITH A CHICKEN
By Eloise Coleman

On my vacation I visited with my gran parents in Iowa and my gran father learned me dont get perconel with a chicken. My gran father has a few chickens and one was a chicken I got perconel with and gave the name Gene Autry. One day my gran mother deside to have stood chicken for dinner and says Orf you go out and kill a hen meening my gran father. I went with him and low and behole he took a pole with a wire on the end and reeched in the pen and got Gene Autry by the leg and pulled him out and before I cood say a werd he rung his neck wich pulls off his hed and he flops around on the grond back and forth without no hed on and I cryed. He was a brown one. Then he scalted him in hot water and picket the feathers of and saw me crying and says dont ever get perconel with a chicken. When we are at the dinner table he says it again so I ate some, a drumb stick. I dident say anything but it was like eating my own rellatives. So dont get perconel with a chicken, also a cow if you are going to eat it later on. Also a caff.

Our next juvenile author describes herself as "11 yrs old, have terrible penmenship, modern, tall and ambitious." The terrible penmenship she has makes me uncertain about her last name, which is Gillers, or Gellers, or Gellus, or Gillus, or Humperdinck. Her first name is Marilyn and her essay follows:

AMERICA'S FAULTS

To begin with you must remember the fact that I am from Florida (Ft.-Lauderdale to be exact) so this is only Ft. Laud's viewpoint.

Some people believe that we are ruining our beautiful Land O Plenty by putting up factories, changing old-fashioned villages to thriving Metropolesons, and wanting to make beautiful forests to rocket test areas.

I have nothing against this except I will stay on Earth when everybodys up on Mars or the Moon.

And as far as factories, put them up by all means IF (the all important word) they found a way to ABOLISH SMOG.

Fred Beck stands as authority for a story about a little girl who went to visit her aunt. The little girl had been raised in a heathen household but her Aunt Elsie was a righteous woman, and sent the child to Sunday School. There she was given the first Sunday School card she had ever seen. She wrote home:

Dear Daddy,
 Aunt Elsie sent me to Sundy school and the kids sang hims and then they gave me an ad for heaven.
                                        love Beatrice

When Randy Jacob of Yardley, Pennsylvania, was eight years old his grandfather wanted the boy to develop an interest in nature and outdoor things. So he told Randy to go out and observe nature, and then write about it, and if the stuff he wrote was good, he would be given some money. Randy's first submission follows:

BUGS AND INSECTS OF ALL KINDS
The spider is not an insect. It has 8 legs. Some people call it an insect when it is a plain bug. It is a pest to most people for it makes big cobwebs in corners of walls and other places and leaves it. Some people are even afraid of it.
 The Yellowjacket is another stinging insect, it is a lot like the bee only smaller. It seems like it is meant for stinging because it has no other use. A bee makes honey, a wasp just walks around enjoying life, and hardly ever does any flying, but a yellowjacket seems to fly around stinging people on purpose.

Randy got his money for that essay because he was a good writer even when he was eight years old. At that same time, he edited a little newspaper in which he demonstrated a sure talent for writing humor. Witness this "news item" from the *Forest City Times of Animalland*:

PUTTOKOSKY SYMPHONY CONDUCTOR
DIES OF ASTHMA ON STAGE

FOREST CITY: At Colton Hall yesterday there was a concert with the Puttokosky Orchestra. It was the second of a series of concerts with Lawrence Lizard conducting. While they were playing his favorite theme in Ombedalt's Symphony No. 3, Mr. Lizard collapsed on the floor. He was conducting very vigorously at the time. He had become short of breath.

One of the players in the orchestra saved the panic-stricken audience by quickly dropping his instrument, getting up and snatching the baton. He shouted to the orchestra to play the national anthem and conducted them several times thru the piece so the audience had to stand at attention. Then he shouted to the orchestra to continue, turned to the microphone and said, "Ladies and gentlemen, please be calm. This is only a slight case of stage fright, but the concert will not continue. Will everyone please leave the building so we may examine Mr. Lizard. Thank you for being with us. Goodbye. The player hadn't felt of his pulse yet. Later they found he was dead. Afterwards they found out he had had asthma for several years.

His funeral will be tomorrow.

He died at 3:23 P. M. April 22, 1951, A. C.

But I'll bet when he goes down in history they will say that he died at the fourth measure of the first theme, the 23rd measure of the 3rd movement of Symphony No. 3 by Charles Porcupine Ombedalt.

The writing in the above epic, according to certain amateur authorities on children, is just a trifle too slick for an eight-year-old. These authorities say that Randy's work has been severely edited by an older person — that a child of eight, for one thing, could never make it through that much prose without a few misspelled words. However, Randy's mother says he wrote it, and I'm not one to dispute a mother when she's talking about her own offspring.

Once at the *New York Herald Tribune* a certain book for children arrived in the office and it was decided to hand it over to a twelve-year-old for review. The child wrote one of the shortest reviews on record, yet one of the most perceptive in the whole history of literary criticism — a commentary that could be applied to many another book. It follows:

This book is very good but too long in the middle.

Following publication of *Write Me a Poem, Baby,* some of my neighbors became more conscious of their children's writings than they had been in the past. One little girl was allowed to stay up Election Night and watch the excitement on television. Afterward, her mother suggested that she write her impressions of the election. She did. She wrote a poem:

> Clack clack
> Went the univac.

It seems improbable that Elizabeth Anne Rout, a Canadian girl, ever saw the vaudeville team of Smith & Dale performing their famous Dr. Kronkhite act. Yet Elizabeth Anne wrote a play when she was nine years old, and as I read it I had a strange feeling that I was listening to Smith & Dale. The play follows:

THE SOLVED PROBLEM

This sean begins in a pacuilure way. It starts with a begger sitting under a tree humming. It might not seem funny but its funny akording to the title.

BEGGER	(hum) (walk downtown) Sits down play vilen.
LADY	Would you like me to help you.
BEGGER	No thanks but its very kind of you to ask.
LADY	Well why are you playing a vilen.
BEGGER	What vilen.
LADY	The one in your hand.
BEGGER	Oh I'm beggeing.
LADY	Well when I ask you would you like me to help you, you said no thanks.

BEGGER	No I didn't because you didn't ask me.
LADY	Yes I did — You had better come to the docter with me.
BEGGER	What Dr.
LADY	Never mind what Dr. just come.
BEGGER	Come where.
LADY	Look don't be silly — just come.
BEGGER	Come where.
LADY	To the Drs.
NARRATOR	They are now at last in the Drs. Office.
DR.	What can I do for you.
LADY	Could you please test this man.
DR.	Where do you want me to test him.
LADY	All over the place please — because I do not no what is wrong.
DR.	He'll have to go to the hospotill.
LADY	Is it all right begger.
BEGGER	Yes.
NAR.	There all at the hospotill.
DR.	There is this a nice bed.
BEGGER	Yes very nice.
NURCE	Its time for your opperation.
BEGGER	What opperation.
NURCE	I can't explane now.
NAR.	The nurce & the lady are speaking together.
NURCE	Is that the truble with him.
LADY	Yes
NURCE	I'll fix that soon. — Docter.
DR.	Yes.
NURCE	You have to repeat everything to him thats the truble.

DR.	We can fix that soon.
NAR.	Soon he was all better and everyone was visiting him.
MARY	Oh hello Frank its so nice to see you I hope your out of the hospetil soon.
GEORGE	How do you feel Frank, have a nice Christmas.
NAR.	And I'd like to tell you the begger married the lady and they lived happley ever after.
ALLTOGETHER	MERRY CHRISTMAS AND A HAPPY NEW YEAR.

When Johnnie Choate was nine years old he was given a writing assignment at school. He was told to read the old English ballad, *Lord Ullin's Daughter*, and then to tell the story in his own words. Let us first have a look at what Johnnie wrote:

"Sandy" called Lord Ullin, Bring My daughter to me". Yes Sire said Sandy. "Come come my daughter I will take you to a castle wich we mite by. "O father you are always beying things. wy don't you think of the poor for a change."

"O phhooy to the poor they should earn there money instead of beging for it."

"Father your so very crule.

"Why daughter you speak souch bad talk"

"It is very right what I say and speachy you saying

boo to the poor. Why you ought to be a shamed of your shelf. Im going to run away.

That is as far as Johnnie went with it, and I don't know what his teacher said if he turned it in to her. Right at the beginning, however, there is one small matter to be cleared up — that word "speachy." After much soul-searching I came to the conclusion that Johnnie meant "specially" and his mother verified this.

Now, as to the original ballad — I was not acquainted with it and had to do some digging in the public library, where I found it and read it. One thing is certain — Johnnie didn't copy anything verbatim. In the Campbell ballad Lord Ullin's daughter and the chief of Ulva's Isle are eloping and have been on the road for three days, pursued by Lord Ullin and his men. They have arrived at Lochgyle, and they plead with the ferryman to row them across, and he agrees, and Lord Ullin arrives on the shore just in time to see the boat capsize and his daughter drown. That's all there is to it. Nobody named Sandy. No talk about castles to by. No phhooy to the poor. No daughter speaking souch bad talk. In fact, it appears to me that Johnnie was deeply dissatisfied with the whole plot as set forth by Campbell, even the elopment part. Having real old Campbell's version, I must confess that I'm in agreement.

The most famous work of juvenilia in modern times is *The Young Visiters* by Daisy Ashford. This stirring and romantic novel was written about 1900 by a nine-year-old English girl, using a pencil and a cheap notebook. When it was finally published it carried a laudatory preface by James M. Barrie. It created quite a sensation and it was so funny, so expertly contrived, that some critics charged Barrie with writing it himself. Its authenticity was soon established; and the last I heard its author, now Mrs. James Devlin, was living on a farm near Norwich. She is still collecting royalties from her childhood work (a handsome new edition of *The Young Visiters* was published by Doubleday & Company in 1951, illustrated by William Pène du Bois). It has had a continuing popularity, I think, because it mirrors so accurately the attitudinizing of the adult English world in the time of a somewhat mildewed queen.

The book tells the story of Mr. Salteena, Ethel Monticue, and Bernard Clark. To put it briefly, Mr. Salteena was in love with Ethel, but he had high social ambitions and when he went off to pursue them, he left Ethel in the care of his friend Bernard Clark. We have space here for only two passages. The first of these tells of the arrival of Mr. Salteena and Ethel at the residence of Bernard.

THE FIRST EVENING

When they had unpacked Mr Salteena and Ethel
went downstairs to dinner. Mr. Salteena had put on a
compleat evening suit as he thought it was the correct
idear and some ruby studs he had got at a sale. Ethel
had on a dress of yellaw silk covered with tulle which
was quite in the fashion and she had on a necklace
which Mr Salteena gave her for a birthday present. She
looked very becomeing and pretty and Bernard heaved
a sigh as he gave her his arm to go into dinner. The
butler Minnit was quite ready for the fray standing up
very stiff and surrounded by two footmen in green
plush and curly white wigs who were called Charles and
Horace.

Well said Mr Salteena lapping up his turtle soup
you have a very sumpshous house Bernard.

His friend gave a weary smile and swallowed a few
drops of sherry wine. It is fairly decent he replied with
a bashful glance at Ethel after our repast I will show
you over the premisis.

Many thanks said Mr Salteena getting rarther flus-
tered with his forks.

You ourght to give a ball remarked Ethel you have
such large compartments.

Yes there is room enough sighed Bernard we might
try a few steps and meanwhile I might get to know a
few peaple.

So you might responded Ethel giving him a speaking
look.

Mr Salteena was growing a little peevish but he
cheered up when the Port wine came on the table and

the butler put round some costly finger bowls. He did not have any in his own house and he followed Bernard Clark's advice as to what to do with them. After dinner Ethel played some merry tunes on the piano and Bernard responded with a rarther loud song in a base voice and Ethel clapped him a good deall. Then Mr Salteena asked a few riddles as he was not musicle. Then Bernard said shall I show you over my domain and they strolled into the gloomy hall.

I see you have a lot of ancesters said Mr Salteena in a jelous tone, who are they.

Well said Bernard they are all quite correct. This is my aunt Caroline she was rarther exentrick and quite old.

So I see said Mr Salteena and he passed on to a lady with a very tight waist and quearly shaped. That is Mary Ann Fudge my grandmother I think said Bernard she was very well known in her day.

Why asked Ethel who was rarther curious by nature.

Well I dont quite know said Bernard but she was and he moved away to the next picture. It was of a man with a fat smiley face and a red ribbon round him and a lot of medals. My great uncle Ambrose Fudge said Bernard carelessly.

He looks a thourough ancester said Ethel kindly.

Well he was said Bernard in a proud tone he was really the Sinister son of Queen Victoria.

Not really cried Ethel in excited tones but what does that mean.

Well I dont quite know said Bernard Clark it puzzles me very much but ancesters do turn quear at times.

The story buzzes along rarther briskly, and Ethel arrives at the point where she has to tell Mr Salteena she doesn't love him.

This is agony cried Mr Salteena clutching hold of a table my life will be sour grapes and ashes without you.

Thus the stage is set for one of the great romantic passages of English literature, the chapter titled "A Proposale," which follows:

Next morning while imbibing his morning tea beneath his pink silken quilt Bernard decided he must marry Ethel with no more delay. I love the girl he said to himself and she must be mine but I somehow feel I can not propose in London it would not be seemly in the city of London. We must go for a day in the country and when surrounded by the gay twittering of the birds and the smell of the cows I will lay my suit at her feet and he waved his arm wildly at the gay thought. Then he sprang from bed and gave a rat tat at Ethels door.

Are you up my dear he called.

Well not quite said Ethel hastilly jumping from her downy nest.

Be quick cried Bernard I have a plan to spend a day near Windsor Castle and we will take our lunch and spend a happy day.

Oh Hurrah shouted Ethel I shall soon be ready as I had my bath last night so wont wash very much now.

No dont said Bernard and added in a rarther fervent

tone through the chink of the door you are fresher than the rose my dear no soap could make you fairer.

Then he dashed off very embarrased to dress. Ethel blushed and felt a bit excited as she heard the words and she put on a new white muslin dress in a fit of high spirits. She looked very beautifull with some red roses in her hat and the dainty red ruge in her cheeks looked quite the thing. Bernard heaved a sigh and his eyes flashed as he beheld her and Ethel thorght to herself what a fine type of manhood he reprisented with his nice thin legs in pale broun trousers and well fitting spats and a red rose in his button hole and rarther a sporting cap which gave him a great air with its quaint check and little flaps to pull down if necessary. Off they started the envy of all the waiters.

They arrived at Windsor very hot from the jorney and Bernard at once hired a boat to row his beloved up the river. Ethel could not row but she much enjoyed seeing the tough sunburnt arms of Bernard tugging at the oars as she lay among the rich cushons of the dainty boat. She had a rarther lazy nature but Bernard did not know of this. However he soon got dog tired and sugested lunch by the mossy bank.

Oh yes said Ethel quickly opening the sparkling champaigne.

Dont spill any cried Bernard as he carved some chicken.

They eat and drank deeply of the charming viands ending up with merangs and choclates.

Let us now bask under the spreading trees said Bernard in a passiunate tone.

Oh yes lets said Ethel and she opened her dainty

parasole and sank down upon the long green grass. She closed her eyes but she was far from asleep. Bernard sat beside her in profound silence gazing at her pink face and long wavy eye lashes. He puffed at his pipe for some moments while the larks gaily caroled in the blue sky. Then he edged a trifle closer to Ethels form.

Ethel he murmured in a trembly voice.

Oh what is it said Ethel hastily sitting up.

Words fail me ejaculated Bernard horsly my passion for you is intense he added fervently. It has grown day and night since I first beheld you.

Oh said Ethel in supprise I am not prepared for this and she lent back against the trunk of the tree.

Bernard placed one arm tightly round her. When will you marry me Ethel he uttered you must be my wife it has come to that I love you so intensely that if you say no I shall perforce dash my body to the brink of yon muddy river he panted wildly.

Oh dont do that implored Ethel breathing rarther hard.

Then say you love me he cried.

Oh Bernard she sighed fervently I certinly love you madly you are to me like a Heathen god she cried looking at his manly form and handsome flashing face I will indeed marry you.

How soon gasped Bernard gazing at her intensly.

As soon as possible said Ethel gently closing her eyes.

My Darling whispered Bernard and he seiezed her in his arms we will be marrid next week.

Oh Bernard muttered Ethel this is so sudden.

No no cried Bernard and taking the bull by both

horns he kissed her violently on her dainty face. My bride to be he murmered several times.

Ethel trembled with joy as she heard the mistick words.

Oh Bernard she said little did I ever dream of such as this and she suddenly fainted into his out stretched arms.

Oh I say gasped Bernard and laying the dainty burden on the grass he dashed to the waters edge and got a cup full of the fragrant river to pour on his true loves pallid brow.

She soon came to and looked up with a sickly smile Take me back to the Gaierty hotel she whispered faintly.

With plesure my darling said Bernard I will just pack up our viands ere I unloose the boat.

Ethel felt better after a few drops of champagne and began to tidy her hair while Bernard packed the remains of the food. Then arm in arm they tottered to the boat.

I trust you have not got an illness my darling murmured Bernard as he helped her in.

Oh no I am very strong said Ethel I fainted from joy she added to explain matters.

Oh I see said Bernard handing her a cushon well some people do he added kindly and so saying they rowed down the dark stream now flowing silently beneath a golden moon. All was silent as the lovers glided home with joy in their hearts and radiunce on their faces only the sound of the mystearious water lapping against the frail vessel broke the monotony of the night.

So I will end my chapter.

[83]

Maxine Morris tells of the time her grandchildren came for Thanksgiving Day, bringing along the toy printing set that had just been given to Robbie, age seven. Robbie was in a quandary: he had a printing set and he couldn't think of anything to print! So Maxine suggested that he do the place cards for the twelve people who would be present for Thanksgiving dinner. It then became necessary for her to explain at some length the nature and function of place cards, and after that Robbie retired to another room and went to work. He was a long time at the job and the table had been set when he finally finished, so he distributed the cards at the places. When Maxine came to inspect his work, she found that each card bore the same word: Y O U.

The wife of a leading New York movie critic came home late one afternoon and was greeted by the cook with this: "I didn't let nobody dig because nobody come to dig." Confusion reigned. Then the cook brought forth a note which had been written by the young son of the house and placed on the kitchen table. It said:

Elizabeth:
    if any one comes and says he wants to dig on are property tell them no. if they do dig call at this number

Wi7-5128. REMEMBER dont let them talk you into it
not even if they say they have per mission

Jeff

Nobody came to dig because nobody had been
asked to come to dig, and nobody had threatened that
they were coming to dig. Jeff just made the whole
thing up. Without per mission.

The "Trade Winds" department of the *Saturday Review* recently published a book criticism written by a
boy in Toledo, Ohio. The book was titled *Street Rod*
and the Toledo lad sent his review to the publisher,
Bantam Books. It follows:

> I have just read your book "Street Rod." I just think
> the book is horrible. Oh sure it was okay at the begin-
> ning but it was pretty darn lousy at the end. Link
> slaughtered Ric in two fights and beat him in every
> drag race. I guess you expect Ricky to sit around suck-
> ing his thumb. He did what I or any other decent man
> would have done he fought back. I am 12 years old
> which you may not think as very much but I think I've
> got a right to make a complaint if I have one. Ricky
> worked hard and won the trophy but what about all
> the nagging he took when he started the DTA club and
> couldn't go rodding with the other guys.
>
> Instead of getting payed back some way Ricky gets
> killed in his own dream car. Including his girl friend.

Oh yeah you're thinking well he was a show-off when he first got his rod. You may be thinking "well it's only a story." Go ahead say its just a story but how would you like to dream about cars all your life then get killed in your "dream rod" while racing a jerk that had been pestering you ever since you had gotten your rod?

At this point I would like to make a brief comment on people who suffer from a virulent affliction, Editor's Head, or Blue Pencilillin. There is something inside most people, a small gland in the left cheek, rear, which gives those people the urge to correct manuscripts. The above book review surely was not composed exactly as it appears here. The Toledo boy sent it to Bantam Books where, no doubt, it passed through several hands. Then it was shoved along to the *Saturday Review* and the people who do "Trade Winds." Somebody along the way, perhaps several somebodies, couldn't keep clumsy hands off of it. They *corrected* it. In the last few years I have been dealing with hundreds and hundreds of manuscripts and letters and notes composed by young children, many of them in the twelve-year-old bracket. I say that the Toledo boy could not have written those two long paragraphs without several misspellings. I doubt very much if he put the apostrophe in "I've" and "it's." I doubt very much if he put a hyphen in "show-off." I doubt very much if he used quotation marks around "Street Rod" and "dream rod" and "well it's only a story." Some twerp undergoing a seizure of Editor's Head at Bantam or at the *Saturday Review* did those things. In so doing, they took away a great deal of the charm of the boy's little essay. It happens that in many cases I have had a chance to examine compositions by school children as they were actually scribbled on the paper; and then I've seen them after the teacher got through correcting them. In every case the editing destroyed the intrinsic merit of the writing. In some cases a classic disappeared. As long as we are talking about sending people to the moon, let us be sensible about it. Let us send editors.

Mrs. Maurine C. Grau tells me that when she was a teacher an eighth-grader did a magnificent summary of the Arthurian legend in verse, as follows:

> There was a young Knight
>   Named Lancelot
> He loved Queen Gwinevere
>   An Awful lot.
> King Arthur got wise and said
> "Listen you guys,
>   Somebody's going to get shot."

When Cassy Espy was much younger than she is today, she decided to organize her affairs, to lead an orderly existence. To this end she went in for single-entry bookkeeping so that she might always know where she stood financially. Her mother has passed along a page from Cassy's account book, as follows:

Candy   3
gum   5
ribben 15
All toll   23

The mother of little Martha Driggs, of Easton, Pennsylvania, has searched high and low without finding a short story written by Martha — which, I feel sure, would have been worth publishing here. All Mrs. Driggs can remember about it is the title: MER-GENCY WARD.

One spring afternoon when she was about seven, Mona Espy was sitting in the yard when a sudden surge of religious feeling hit her. She hurried into the house, got pencil and paper, and wrote as follows:

I Love you God I Love you so much that I wish that I was in the aire. to god. by mona.

Paul Nathan, who writes for *Publishers' Weekly*, served as one of the judges in a sixth-grade essay contest. All of the children wrote on the subject "Courtesy, the Art of Being Nice," and Mr. Nathan's favorite — though not the winner — was this one:

Courtesy can help us mentally, for it leaves us with a free conchonce & a happy soul. Courtesy has helped us win wars. Suppose the U. S. is being beaten in a war of missles by Russia. Briton chimes in & we soon beat Russia. They did this kind deed for they knew we could help them too.

Courtesy can save money & lives too. Imagine that Ichabod is driving in the suburbs of a large establishment. Having smoked a cigar, he flicks it out the window. Ichabod's cigar started a gigantic fire which claimed 3,000,000 lives & just as many dollars damage. By the way, Ichabod's children were killed. He could have stopped this disaster by simply putting the cigar in the ashtray.

Another example . . . Say King Joe is visiting Mongolia. On his way he falls of a cliff, a phesant found him & cured him. In return, the king made the phesant a high official in his court. Also there is the story of the thorn in the lions paw & the boy gets it out so the lion repays him with his life. Courtesy Pays!!!!

A Connecticut couple, owning a pair of girl twins aged eight and named Carol and Clara, allowed the children to spend a week end at the country residence of a couple who had no offspring. Clara appointed herself official chronicler of the expedition and later presented the following report to her parents:

> Mr. Fitzpatrick is deiting he wants to get skinny and look young. Carol gave me an Indin burn and I give her one back. They have an orgen and we practised on it it's easier than the piano. I would practice much on the orgen if we had one. They told us to look at the litning bugs and we did but we have litening bugs in Greenich but we dont look out. Mr. Fizpatrick has a big gardon with corn but the corn is not as tall as our corn and dont grow as fast as our corn. They met in Masschuses Carol ask mr. Fizpatrick who proposed to who and he said mrs. Fizpatrick proposd to him but mrs. fizpatrick said he was a fibre and dont believe a word he says. They drunk ten cans of beer. They have 2 bird feders but not as nice as ours and the skwerels get on them.

The following short story was written by an eleven-year-old girl who lives in Sewickley, Pennsylvania:

S L I M Y
(*Story of a worm*
by Bonnie Roberts)

Slimy was resting on his favorite stone of mosquito larve. He was thinking about the terrible tragedy of 55' when his cousin had been chopped in half by a monstrious hoe. Killed! "Poor old Jud", Slimy was saying to himself when suddenly the earth shook the roots that held the very foundations of his home. A clump of earth was turned over. Eger hands reached out and grabbed Slimy around the middle. This was the terrible fate that his parents had continualy warrned him about. Finally the hands opened dropping the frightened worm into a large box with damp sod in it. Slimy quickly wriggled down into the dirt and was surprised to find that he was not alone. Several other worms, a few of which he knew, were there also, all talking at once. "My dears," exclaimed an especially fat old lady worm, "did you ever see anything like it? The way he dumped us into this cage! It's outrageous I tell you, outrageous."

Slimy crawled around looking for a way to escape. Finding none he turned sadly back to the others, pausing for a moment to talk to a pinchbug, who had found himself in the same predicament. Slimy listened to the moaning of the other worms and suddenly had an idea. He rushed back to the pinchbug and found him sharpening his pincers on a bit of stone. "A splendid idea," said the pinchbug after he had heard Slimy's plan. He ambled over to the edge of the box and began drilling a hole large enough for himself and the other worms to go through. Just as he had finished, the terrible human saw the hole and patched it up with a piece of tape. Suddenly they all felt a jar and the box was lifted. As it was set down a large hole was ripped in the soggy cardboard bottom. Unaware of this the human kept on at his digging. "Now's our chance" thot Slimy. He called to the others to come. They followed him silently deep into the ground and out of reach of human hands. The

[91]

worms and the pinchbug thanked him again and again. He was their hero, and they put his bust in the Worm Hall of Fame next to Joe de Maggot.

When Jackie Pearson, of Silver Spring, Maryland, was five years old she concluded that she had seen enough of life and the world to produce an autobiography. This is the way she dictated it:

STORY OF MY LIFE

Once upon a time there was a little girl and she always went to a corner every day and saw a policeman named Jack. And that policeman was Irish and he was crazy of a little girl. And this little girl's name was Jackie. And she went on to kindergarten by herself. And then she went to nursery school. She ate lunch and took a rest and then her mother came and got her. And then they went home and ate dinner. And then her mother put her to bed. And the next day the same thing over again. That's all.

Mrs. Mamie H. Carter of Troy, Alabama, has sent me a book, excitingly illustrated in color, the work of a little girl named Josephine Blumentritt. The text follows:

ALL ABOUT SWEETNESS
(*Dedicated to Maimie who is sick in bed*)

Once upon a time there lived a little calf named Sweetness.

She really was very sweet. She lived out in the west where a lot of little calfs just like her lived. They wernt just like her though becouse she was a thourbred calf. She had a beautiful mother named Elena Maria Elexis of Greendale. Her mother was a very famous champion. She had a solid gold bell around her neck. She won it in a show. Here is her father. His name is "Sir Lancerlot Alexis of Greedale Farms."

She was very sad because she hated to do everything she had to.

She would have loved to eat the nice green grass like other little calfs did . . . but insted — she had to stand in a stall all day and eat nice fresh hay with vitamins in it and sacks of specially mixed feed. Poor poor Sweetness!

She would have loved to drink the cool water from the stream in the woods like other calves did but insted . . . she had to drink water that was colored. The colour was supposed to help her grow. Poor poor Sweetness!

She would have loved to roll over and over in the dust but insted . . . her straw was changed every one hour and she was brushed and her tail put in curlors every three hours. Poor poor Sweetness.

One day a friend of hers (a old bull) came walking down by her stall (being led of course).

Where are you going asked Sweetness?

Oh I am going to the slaughter house everybody'll go there before long.

Ohhh answered Sweetness.

A year later a man came and started to put on a halter Sweetness was very sad because now she would have

[93]

to die in the slaughter house. The man was very happy.

But insted of going to anything like a slaughter house she went out in a yard with a very handsome bull.

So she spent the day with him and at night she went home.

Three months later Sweetness her name was now Maria Sweetness of Greendale had a sweet baby calf and she named it Mary.

P.S. Sweetness was very happy that her child could have everything that she wanted. So that Mary grew up to be a very beautiful cow. Here is Mary's picture (with her calf when she grew up).

THE END

Mrs. Cora McLain, a teacher on Long Island, sends me a brief essay by a six-year-old girl reporting on her first airplane trip:

The plane was silver the stewdess on the plane served us are dinner and daddy and mamma wiskey. She is beautifel and wore a blew dress and little lite blew cap and a nice figuer. She said we are over Pitsberg if you want to look out. They had emerjency exis if you are recked and also little bags to throw up in. The desert was apple pie with chese.

A sixth-grade history teacher in Illinois was instructing her pupils in the life and times of Alfred the Great. The textbook they were using included the legend of the cakes. King Alfred, fleeing after his defeat at Chippenham, took refuge in a peasant's hut. The housewife, not recognizing him in his rags, put him to watching some cakes that were baking by the fire. He was so absorbed in his meditations that he allowed the cakes to burn and was scolded as an idle and useless wretch.

There was one boy in the class who was so impressed by this story that he could remember nothing else about Alfred the Great. So when the time came for the children to write essays on the subject of Alfred, the teacher said: "Now please don't put down the story of Alfred and the cakes — I'm tired of hearing about it." A short while later the boy turned in his paper. His essay:

> One day when Alfred the Great was wandering about the country side, he stopped at the house of a certin lady, but the lease said about that the better.

On assignment a child in the famous Little Red School House in New York City turned in the following:

MY THREE WISHES
First of all, I want a horse to ride on, with a fancy outfit besides a saddle and bridle. Then I want to be a famous TV actress so when I come off the stage I will receive boquets. I want a duplex on Park Avenue with ten kittens in it.

In 1957 the *PAL News*, published by the famous Police Athletic League of New York City, sponsored an essay contest in conjunction with the National Book Committee. PAL children of all ages participated, writing brief pieces on the subject, *Why I Like to Read Books*.

Through the courtesy of Miss Joy Chute I was permitted to go through several hundred of these essays. It turned out to be an exhilarating and even inspiring experience for a person who writes books himself. Why do children read books? One wrote, "Reading is a good exersise for the eyes." Another mentioned his ambitions: "I want to be one of Two Things. Be the head of my own orphanize or write books. The person who thought of books made a great step for the world."

One boy said that if you read books "you can go with Bufflo Bill as he chases Bufflo." Another that "you can learn all about God and Bugs Bunny." A third observed, "Some of the stories show interesting word like murder and dead."

A girl said she enjoyed books because they taught her about "the launcheing of the Russian Satelite (sputniek) by the Russian." And a boy gave a forthright, beautiful reason for reading: "Books teach you to be a good reader and it is very good to be a good reader because then you can read the mail."

I should like to mention one fact that stands out in the PAL papers: children are not able to spell Huckleberry Finn's name correctly. I find it spelled Hukey Berry Fin, Hutchelbary Fin and Hucelberry fin. And among the other titles mentioned in the essays are Robbison Carino, Kid Carson, Davy Crokeet, Poem by Luis Carol, Alice of Wonder Lam, Gunns of Montania and the Legened of Sleepey Hello.

In the section that follows are the PAL essays which I found most interesting.

> Reading is very important because if you dont know how to read you dont know anything like if you wanted to wash the dishes and you wanted to use a clenser and there where two cans you woulden know which one to use. Books teaches you more.

> The best way to obtain knowledge is by reading books. Many books are most interestion, there are many books obtaning auto and biography stories of very important and interesting people, such as Ben Franklin a great inventor, and Abrahan Lincoln the sixth teenth of the United State, and freed the slaves, and was called the "Peac Macker." Books cotain knowledge that is important for school work and social life.

> The most interesting book that I have read is called

"Marco Polo's Adventures." It tells of the trip that Marco Polo took to see Ku Klux Klan. It also tells of the adventures during his stay in Japan and the Oriedent. When Marco Polo visited Ku Klux Klan he was welcomed by the people of Japan. Towards to end of the book Marco Polo had made a friend of Ku Klux Klan and he succeedded in making Japan open to the new world. Don't you think that if you read this book you would say it was interesting and educational? That is why I like to read books, Don't you?

I like reading because it is interesing and it is as beautiful pictures and name of people you learn about in shool. And it help you know your reading. And it is a intresing book if you pick out the right one. We read our book at the liebery or bring them home. You get your card at the liebery.

Murder are the best for grownups. The author of books learn to get to right books by reading them. I don't like to be and author of a book but when maybe you get good at something they may ask you something about it.

I like to read books of interesting animals like bears dears foxs elephant birds lions and tigers and other interesting thing and some day i'll go hunting for these animals to.

Through my reading experients I have met and made a great many new friends. I have fought side by side with the There Musketeers. I sailed down the Missippie with Hucelberry fin. I lived and loved with Lincoln. I have experienced many gay times through reading but I have also fealt sad.

The reason I like to read books is because books have helped me in school very much but thats not the only thing. Books is a help to boys and girls when they have nothing else to do. Books have helped me a lot in these things writing diffrent kinds of stories, history, coumetty work, group reporting and poems. But there's more than one kind of book. There is a Comic Book. I like comic books very much they are very funny books. But there are comic books that are not funny. These books are only spooky, horror, that's only some of them kind of books, but here is another kind robbing, killing, fighting, shooting, baseball, football, horseracing, trackrunning, and basketball. And there is another kind of exlent book Readers Digest. Now that kind of book we get in school every mounth.

Think about this questions? Does reading a lot improve your reading skills? Does reading help you prounce words?

I use to go to a special reading class two years ago. At first I didn't like reading but know I love to read. In reading class I learnt how to prounce my words. When I read a books like Schlock Homes, Mark Saber, and etc. I know something on their field of work. I like to read comic books more then any other kind of books.

I like to read books because it is a fine past time and on a rainy day and I am not allowed out all I have to do is to get a book that I think I will enjoy and set down and read it. Books can also help you in your studys for instance if you don't know the meaning of a word all you have to do is to look up the Dictionary and find the correct meaning of the word your stuck on. realy a person that is interrested in books is not a book worm like people say and the truth is anybody that is interrested in books is always smart Because there is more knowledge in one book than there is in five people.

One day I was talking to my farther about a certain book the Bewitched Caverns. My father told me to go to the libary and to ask the liberian where to find it. When I did find it the first couple of pages were very good. But the kind of name the cave men had such name as olo, Pigeon, and snake-head. Olo fell off a cliff he thoght it was the evil spirits that had trip him but it realy was a vine. When he was falling sharp things were sticking into him. When he reached the bottom he was onconscience. A girl named pigeon had saw him fall she ran over to him to see if he was dead or alive. He was still alive she got a piece of rage and wet it she put it on his forehead. And he regained conscience. He was very dizzy from the fall he walked to her cave were she was living. And they lived happly everafter.

Dictionaries, Encyclopedias and many more books give information. Telephone books give information. We usually get our fun out of comic books. Older people get thiers out of dramas. There are even books to tell you how to write books. There are books for all ages including babies. There are books that have pomes, rymes, riddles, jokes, and etc. Books have words that express the real meaning of the story. Good books are easy to understand if the author knows what he is writing. Why don't you just pick up a pencil and paper and start writing a book.

Some books tell of jungel men exploring the African jungle and of all the adventure and dangerous acts they do while setting traps for diffrent animals so people in the city can see them in the zoo.

While other books contain something like a big smart brain that nows much about everything. for example the very smart Encyclopedia in which you can find about diffrent words or things in the world. Much information is kept in these books from men who have studded much to write them.

Other books are funny and ful of enjoyment. For it tells of rediculas characters which play the part in a makebelieve land. Especaly ferry tails. They tell of diffrent people wich go on voyages and have ship recks and enter strange lands in which animls talk and live like people. But it always ends with the people leaving the lands of makebelieve and telling the tails to their friends.

Books, Books, Books. That's all you can hear in school but when you grow up you'll be thankful you had the chance.

I like to read Books about the Saints And thir way of life. Did you ever Hear of St Terase of Avla. she was the Saint who liked to read. I like to know theas little facts about the Saints. Because if I ever Get sick I can think about the book I have read.

Thease are some of the interesting Facts I learned about Saint Terase she liked to read book about the Saints. At the age of twenty Terase entared the Carmelite Convent. When she was older she wrote her own life the Pater Noster and the interior Castle. When she was dying she said "O my Lord now the time for us to see you" her feast day Oct fifteenth.

Reading books is one of my favorit subjects. By reading you can learn Many things, forinstins all about History and Geography and many more subjects. Moust of the world's smartist men and weman lern by reading books. I myself aren't that type. I like to read faritalls and books about the old days. But one of my favorits are books about famous men in basball. all these men like Babe Ruth, Tie Cobe and other famous men are put into books so many people can read about them.

When Christopher Allen Goodfellow of Detroit was five years old he announced to his mother that the Muse in Charge of Cowboy Composition had touched him and that he wanted to dictate a story. This is precisely how it went:

THE TEXAS RANGER AND LAURA

She saves me from a terrible trap. It is a hole in the ground with brush piled on top. Then when I get out of the trap I see bad men trailing the stage coach. We go to stop them. After we get them we bring them to the sheriff. Then we find the others. They are in their deadly own shack. When we get there we put our horses up to the corral, then we go in. Laura doesn't because she isn't strong enough.

They get us before we get them. We happen to be magic and we raise our hands down but the bad men can't see our arms go down or our guns. Then we bring our sheriff. (They happen to have a telephone in the shack).

The Public Field Librarian for a large Eastern state is a young woman who holds a Master's Degree in Library Science. She doesn't know it but her mother has sent me a bit of her literary work, produced in a school competition when she was eight years old. It is noteworthy because of the rhyming scheme, and it follows:

CARMEL CANDY
Carmel candy, carmel candy!
It sure is fine and dandy!
    It's pritty and neet,
    It sticks to your teet,
Carmel candy, carmel candy!
I always have it handy.

The presence of a typewriter in a home almost always brings out the creative urge in children. Usually they are content to produce a few lines or a few pages of nonsense, but not Mona Espy. Once she got the hang of her mother's typewriter, she went right to work composing her first novel. By good fortune I have the complete manuscript, and here it is:

[103]

Molly-lou jumped out of bed — something filled her mined what was it? oh — she cried now I rember I am going to dance the ballet number in the school auttorem. TOday Mollylou was 18-years old. she grabbed her pink robe with blue lineing and her pink slippers. Mollylou softley tiptoed down stairs because she knew that her mother and father were still asleep it was so early. when she got down she saw there cook Rosley Brown.. Hello there Rose she cried I am . . . . hello honey said Roseley looking up from doing some mixture for pancakes. What are you so exited about? oh Rosley don,t YOU KNOW? I . . . . my own SELF is going to dance in school. Please may I get my own breakfast? why of corse dear your not a baby are you? your 18 today arn,t you? okey Rosley I,ll get some cerel. . . Mollylou was a pretty sort of girl. . . . . she had black hair it was long but yet not to long. it was about 5 inches below her sholders she had a dark complecshon and brown eyes she wore dark litish lipstick. Mollylou was a sweet girl yes very sweet indeed. she heard Mother's sweet voise coming from outside the door. Molly darling could you come here for a minuite?? yes Mother exuse me for a second Rosley I'll be right back. Molly darling I'm so sorry your Father fell down on one of the slippery rugs and I think he has broken his leg. oh oh oh Mollylou cried I'll call a doctor. No Molly dear what I'm worried about is you. no Mother please I don't care about ME all I care about is Father's broken leg I don't care if I don't get to dance in the college school. that's a very thoutful girl Molly darling of course you may.

Father Mollylou asked the next day how do you feel? fine especially with you here said Father. oh Father your onley fooling Mollylou said. oh no Molly I'm not fooling he said. you were very kind and thoutful to stay home and not do that pretty dance of yours. oh ho oh ho Molly cried you think that I can dance prettyily??? Molly Father asked a few minuits later. . . . . don't you want to help Mother with the dishes? O. K. Father you rest back for 20 minuites like a good boy said Mollylou. Hi Mother Mollylou said as she entered the kitcen. oh hello darling Mother said looking toward the door. Mother I told Father to rest for 20 minuites. now I want to help you do the dishes. thank you Molly said Mother. 30 minuites later Mollylou and Mother were finished. Molly tiptoed around to Father's room and went softley into it. there was Father asleep. Mother Fathers asleep said Marylou when she had tiptoed into the livingroom where Mother was looking at collers magizine. thats good she said smiling at Mollylou. oh I forgot to tell you she cried happily looking up a few minuites later. you got a letter from college saying that they didn't have the dance on a count that it was to hot. they are going to have it in a week. oh Mother wonderful Mollylou shouted how wonderful. a hour later Mollylou crept into her Fathers room and she saw that her Father was sitting up in bed reading a book. hi Father she cried want to hear some good news? why Mollylou said Father what is it? Dad I still am going to dance the ballay dance. how do you feel? just fine the pain is complety gone. I'm so glad your going to dance again.

On monday a week later Molly was dressed up in her
balley costume. there was her Father standing up putting his necktie on. hi honey he shouted I'm all better
see??? he stamped his foot down to show her that it
did not hurt. Mollylou was greeted at college by a boy
named Tom just like her Fathers name and that's
what she liked about him. Tom she shouted hi there.
hi sweet cakes he said. Tom stop calling me that name
Mollylou said. I can't help it swee. . . . . Tom STOP
it she cried. gee I realy can't help it because you ARE
just plain SWEET.

THE END

There are several things that confuse me about the
story of Mollylou. In CAPTER II, for example, we
find that Mother has been opening Mollylou's personal mail. If I know anything about girls (and I
don't), that would have precipitated a knock-down-
dragout fight, with Mollylou finally shouting: "I wish
to God I had never been born into this insane family!"
However, that is a small quibble. The overall tone of
the story is what interests me. For a while I thought
the author was registering her own personal protest
against the Beat Generationish literature of today.
Then I realized that this story had been composed before the Beat Generation got beat; the story dates itself by the fact that Mother is looking at collers magazine (although it *could* have been a real old issue of

collers). No — the thing that is wrong is that the story is just too damn sweet, and Mollylou is just too accommodating to everybody. Through a conference with the author's mother I think I found out the answer. The story was written two weeks before Christmas. And this brings us to a whole new field of juvenile literature: the highly moral and sometimes religious tale that is produced, at Christmastime, with what may be a deeply ulterior motive.

The ten-year-old daughter of one of my neighbors turns into a wily conniver as Christmas approaches. Last year her craftiness took a literary bent. About two weeks before Christmas she produced a manuscript bordered with little stickers depicting angels in various angelic postures:

THATS THE CHRISTMAS SPIRIT

Mary Parker could hardly wait till Christmas. It was a month away but still her mind was completley on Christmas. One cold morning on the first of December Mary was sitting on the hearth warming herself. She had just been out in the cold. She suddenly looked over at her father who was busy at his desk writing business letters. Daddy she said why is it that we never see angles? I don't know her father answered I guess it's because they prefer staying up in heaven and what makes you ask such a question? I don't know answered Mary, but I should like to see one. Her father looked at her in a puzzeld way. Then he said don't worry

about such things. He turned back to his work. Mary
had grown tired of sitting still so she got up and ran
into the kitchen where her mother was washing dishes.
Hellow Mary Dear her mother said. Say if my ears
are'nt betraying me I think I heard you and your
father talking about angles. What brought that up?
Oh I don't know Mom its just I've been thinking of
Christmas so much lately. Her Mother hugged her. Its
write around the corner honey she said but what made
you say you would like to see one? Only because I
would Mary asured her.

There is a type of juvenile literature which some
people might find exasperating but which fascinates
me no end. I refer to the story which gets off to a good
start and then comes to an abrupt ending, possibly because the author is bored with it. I have accumulated
many such stories, and they seem to be, almost always,
the work of girls. Sometimes something happens to a
girl author in the middle of a story (even in the middle
of a sentence) and she just gets up and walks away
from it.

I would now like to present two such stories, from
their original manuscripts. I don't know who wrote
them. The first is:

MINTA MARCELLO
Chapter I — The Fatefull Hours
All was quite in the hospital waiting room. Only the

ocasional crackle of a newspaper page as it was being turned was heard. Jose Marcello slammed the magazine down the newspaper he had been trying despritly to concentrate on. He got up and walked over to the far side of the room where a young nurse stood chatting with an elderey woman. "Nurse" he said "How long do it take, any way? Why dont I hear something." The nurse smiled at him. "Mr. Marcello" she said "This is undoubtedly the seventh time youve asked me that in the past hour. It takes a little time to have a baby Mr. Marcello.

"All the time thats what I hear a little time," the young mexican flashed his eyes angerily. The nurse laughed and shook her head. "Go sit down Mr. Marcello" she said "and try and relax. Hear now I'll get you a seditive." Jose stamped his foot. "Oh no" he said "I dont want no seditive." He turned abruply and strutted back across the floor. The nurse shook her head and went on talking to the other woman.

It ends there. No baby. No seditive. No nothing. The second suspenseful tale goes:

A CHRISTMAS STORY

Carol Parker sat on the porch of her little bundalow. She was sad and disturbed. Here it was Christmas Eve and the thermommeter said nindy degrees. There wasn't even a Florida breeze. She couldnt even imagine Santa Clause coming to this hot and dusty place. Carol was only six but knew now to ride a horse as well as a child of thirteen could. She walked over tword the back door of the bundaloe. She looked over the endless plains that rolled as far as her eye could see. Suddenly tears formed in her eyes. She could see New York. She could see the millons of happy faces of people bustling in and out of stores with big packages and bundles. Just then she heard the clop clop of a horses feet as Daddy came riding up to her on the big stallion Sandy. Carol wiped the tears from her eyes but still a unhediable stain stayed around her eyes. Daddy lifted her up on the big stallion and then went in the house. She dident exactly know why but she wanted to get away from this house for

That's the end. What do *you* think? Is she going to light out for New York and all those faces? How far is it to New York? It isn't clear to me whether she's in Florida or Wyoming. The story as it stands has a long way to go, but I'm happy that it got as far as it did, for it has taught me a new word which I'll never forget, namely, unhediable. Unhediable is an adjective and is generally applied to stains. Stains made by tears. On the face. Around the eyes. Of little girls.

Knowing of my interest in juvenilia, the critic Gilbert Highet once recommended that I examine the writings of Marjorie Fleming. "An absolute delight!" said Mr. Highet. Marjorie lived in Scotland a long time ago, and died before she was nine years old.

Robert Louis Stevenson called her "one of the noblest works of God." Sir Walter Scott all but worshiped her. And a hundred years after she died Mark Twain wrote a long appreciation of her, declaring that he had adored her for thirty-six years.

Marjorie Fleming wrote diaries, poems and letters, and I must admit that they are marvelous; yet I contend that many of the modern young authors in this book, and in its predecessor, are just as good as the lass from the Firth of Forth.

Among the passages which her admirers have talked about and written about are the following:

I am now going to tell you about the horrible and wretched plaege that my multiplication gives me you cant concieve it — the most Devilish thing is 8 times 8 and 7 times 7 it is what nature itselfe cant endure.

Miss Potune, a lady of my acquaintance, praises me dreadfully. I repeated something out of Deen Swift & she said I was fit for the stage, & you may think I was primmed up with majestick Pride, but upon my word I felt myself turn a little birsay — birsay is a word which is a word that William composed which is as you may suppose a little enraged. This horrid fat Simpliton says that my Aunt is beautifull which is intirely impossible for that is not her nature . . . Miss Potune is very fat she pretends to be very learned she says she saw a stone that dropt from the skies, but she is a good christian.

In the love novels all the heroins are very desperate Isabella will not allow me to speak about lovers and heroins, and tiss too refined for my taste a loadstone is a curous thing indeed it is true Heroic love doth never win disgrace this is my maxum and I will follow it forever.

My own favorite Marjorie composition is a poem she wrote when she was visiting on a farm. Rats had killed three baby turkeys and the victims were memorialized as follows:

Three turkeys fair their last have breathed
And now this world forever leaved
Their father, and their mother too
They sighed and weep as well as you
Indeed the rats their bones have cranched
Into eternity theire launched
A direful death indeed they had
As wad put any parent mad
But she was more than usual calm
She did not give a single dam.

Mark Twain called Marjorie "the bewitchingest speller and punctuator in all Christendom" and then wrote: "The average child of six 'prints' its correspondence in rickety and reeling Roman capitals, or dictates to mamma, who puts the little chap's message on paper. The sentences are labored, repetitious, and slow; there are but three or four of them; they deal in information solely, they contain no ideas, they venture no judgments, no opinions . . ."

Old Mark Twain was very rarely wrong about anything, but this time I think he goofed; it is obvious that he never examined much of the writing of children in his own day. As I remember the things they wrote, his own daughters were not labored and repetitious and slow, and they didn't lack for ideas and judgments and opinions. Nor do many of the young writers of today. I'd love it if Mark Twain could read the following message, written on a postcard by a six-year-old boy named Gregory Stock. Gregory was in England and his parents, who are from South Africa, were in Paris. This is what he wrote them in script and not Roman capitals:

Dear Mummey and Dadey
    I tolled you not to put sumthing diffrent in the jar in the tadpols I tolled you to put onlie ror meat and bread see you do not listen to me abot tadpols you have killed them Love from Gregory Stock.

And just in case the wraith of Sam Clemens wants further convincing, I have a short short short story written by Diane Cahill, aged eight, of Chicago, in which there is quite clearly an idea, and a judgment on the conduct of women, and an opinion about our civilization, as follows:

One day Dorthy Duck was swimming in the pond. And waddeling along the road was guess who? Dick Duck of coarse. He amed his eye on Dorthy. Hey chick he said how about you and me going swimming in my privet pool? Dorthy trying to egnore him coudn't help to think of a privet pool. So she said, what time? O about seven o'clock tonight. I'll be there said Dorthy. Strange — but the ways of ducks are the same as the ways of people.

Bryan Hamric, a sixth-grader in Dallas, got a B-plus on the following composition which was written as a school assignment and which has been reprinted in both the Dallas *Morning News* and *Time*:

SPRING: AN ESSAY

Spring is my favorite season of the year because we have spring vacation and right after spring vacation we have summer vacation.

When spring comes the weather is much more pleasant and the teachers give us less homework.

In spring lots of tornadoes come and everyone is hoping that one will come and destroy the school. And with the tornadoes comes rain and hail which might flood the city. Then not one person will have to go to school.

Spring is my best season of the year.

Marjorie Fleming may have been the bewitchingest speller of her historical period, but I have a candidate for honors in eccentric orthography, a boy who was writing in the third grade of a Florida school about twenty years ago. His composition has been preserved through the years by his teacher, Mrs. Carl J. Smith, now of New Castle, Delaware, and she has forwarded it to me, advising me to peruse it carefully, for it is *not* written in a foreign language:

A FASH RUNER AND A TUMP-TUMP

Ones a lot of snanks cam apone a Afrcan vilja. The snanks went thu the huts. A fash runer was sent to get the other tribs to help to them to get the snanks away. A big snank was up in a tree not very far away from the vilje in a tree the runer went under the tree the snank was. The big snank fell down on the runer and chocked him to deth. The pepole saw woat happen to the fash runer. Then one man came were the fash runer stan and said way not send the messgn to go by tump-tump. Then a trib a natives came and help trived way the snanks. But the vilja did not loke petter at all.

(Now that I read it over again, and remember that it was written in Jacksonville, I think I may have figured it out. It's Southern dialect, old-fashioned style.)

Back in 1938 a nickel notebook arrived through the mail at the publishing house of Simon and Schuster. It was a novel, called *Roaring Guns*, and the author's name was David Statler. It had all the standard ingredients of the western story: a hero named Tom Mix, a villain named Bill Jhonson, and a heroine named Nomra (possibly Nomra Talmadge?). Upon investigation Mr. Statler turned out to be nine years old. Unable to think of anything else to do, Simon and Schuster called him in, signed a contract with him, and published his book with his own illustrations. Chapter 6, which is titled "TROUBLE," follows:

At dawn Tom and all the rest of the ranch men were very busy. None of the other ranchs knew about the gold mine. Tom and the men did not want them to for fear they would try to rob them so they kept it a secret. Tom loaded his pistol, got a rifle, took a few clean shirts, a few neckerchiefs, and some food. Soon they were ready for actoin and adventure. They all had been in many narrow escapes but they had never been so dangerous. They knew that the Indians would make them trouble for they were not friendly. Here are the names of the men who were going. Tom Mix, Jack Woods, Bob Jhonson, Hoot Gibson, Jhon Kelly, the Boss. They knew the Indians would give them plenty of trouble. So they bought 95 boxes of bullets and 50 rifles. The men who were not going guarded the ranch. Nomra was going too. Tom began to load the bundles into the wagons and then he talked to the boss about their plans. Suddenly there were shots in every corner and men tumbled in every direction. Evidently somebody had found out that they were going to the mine and they wanted to get there first. The ranch caught on fire and every man ran for his life shooting as they ran. Windows were splintering, doors were broken down and the roof, wall, and floor was burning. Suddenly the roof fell in and closed down on the fight. A great storm came up and the wind tore at the roof where the fight was. The fire was burning holes in the roof and as some of them got out of the holes a wind knocked them down. Some of the men maneged to get out. Tom was with them but not for very long because he was lost after while and as he rode along sadly because the adventure of the gold mine was broken up he heard a long pityios wale. Tom galloped in the direction and he saw a wire haired terrier puppy laying on the ground dripping wet and badly scared. Tom jumped off his horse and picked it up and took a clean handkerchief and dried him off. Suddenly he heard voices which were not white mans but Indians! Quickly he hid the puppy and took his horse a little distance off and took the harness and saddle off. Perhaps you wonder why he took the harness and saddle off. Well I'll tell you why he did this. He wanted the horse to look like a wild horse and of course wild horses don't have harness or saddles. Then he dropped down behind a clump of srubbery. He leveled his gun at one man and before you had time to move he was on the ground with a bad wound. The Chief spoke in excited voice "Its the ghost indian me no like him they say he shoot Indians which are good. We shoot too"! A rain of arrows embedded thier sharp points in trees or thickits of bushs and such undergrowth. Tom shot six Indians. He knew they were hostile and of course hostile Indians are not friendly. They took to thier heels as three more of there Indians fell. When the

Indians had gone Tom got up got the dog then mounting his pony he jogged along on his horse. He felt sad because he thoght about the ranch burned up and he wondered where the men he had been lost from were and about the gold mine adventure being found out and ruined. But he found it was no use worrying about it so he hunted the rest of the day trying to find them. Then he went to a hotel called 'New Western.' After he ate his dinner he went to sleep. He woke up that night and heard a noise. As I told you once before he slept with his clothes on. He hurried downstairs and went into a saloon across from the hotel. He saw a drunk man shooting off his guns. Some grim looking men watched him. Tom said to the man "Do you know its aginst the law to get that drunk here in Silver City" Suddenly the drunk man swung his gun to cover Tom. But Tom dived down and tackeled the drunk man and then they got in a death cluth. Tom felt his lungs giving away so he made one desprate jerk at the mans hands which were gripped on his neck but it was no use. Suddenly he gave a stinging blow on the chin on the other man. He loosened the grip then. Tom gave him another one. The man loosend it a little more then Tom with his last burst of strength he sent the man sprawling backwards. But the men who were watching whipped out their guns and sprayed the floor with bullets. Tom got one hand aloose from the other man and whipped out his gun and began to shoot. Some of the men ran to the door, some leaped into the fight, and some let loose smoke and powder. Suddenly the sheriff and some of his men came flying down the street. They leaped off their horses. They entered the saloon with their guns roaring with smoke and flame. The room was filled with the stinging odor of powder and the sheriff and his men and Tom were fighting desprately and surely that they were winning. One after another of the enimies fell blood spattered to the floor. Finally only one man faced Tom, the sheriff and his grim gang. He smashed his fist into one of thems faces and then jerked out his gun and shot a line of fire into the crowd of good men. He struggeled to get aloose and did it. Then he flew down the street. Tom and the sheriff and his men were after him. Tom was at his heels. But the man hit Tom with his mighty arm. Tom gave him a mighty hit on the jaw. The man jerked out his gun and shot at Tom. But Tom ducked it and let his gun rip into the mans side. The man fell dead. Then Tom went back to the hotel and as he opened the door into his room a pistol whissed at him and he saw in his room a gang of ruff bandits. There were ten of them. He whipped out his gun and fired six times as the bandits cracked their guns off. Then they rushed at Tom but a loud voice stopped them and Tom saw standing by the open door Tim Cody! Cody stepped out and swung his gun on the startled crowd of bandits. But suddenly a crowd of bandits who were in the gang of the captured men burst into the room. Some of them set the room on fire, others shot lead at the startled Tom and his partner Tim Cody. Others smashed windows and aimed their guns at some of sheriffs men who were gathered around the hotel. Tom leaped downstairs with a quick jerk his gun was out spitting lead. Smoke filled the streets, the shouts of men were drowned in the gun fire, in every store the men of the sheriffs were dragging dead men out of their windows. Tom leaped into the saddle of his horse Silver and dashed down the road. Tom was on his horse with the bandits after him. Suddenly a milloin Indians rushed at him. The air was thick with arrows, and shots, yells and cries died out over the noise of hoofs, shots, and the clatter of knifes hitting against each other. But the sheriff and his men crashed into actoin and Indians and bandits let up a shout of war and rushed at them. Knifes, guns, axes, clubs, rifles went into actoin. Knifes were shattered into bits, guns were lost, axes were broken, rifles were slpiting into, and men were shouting. Tom jerked a rifle up to his shoulder and began shooting lead in every direction. Men fell to the ground with Toms bullets in their hearts. Tom suddenly saw a man with a 4-5 gun aiming at him over the head of the man went Toms rifle but a crowd of bandits rushed at him and knocked him down. Tom dug his feet into a bandit then he rushed at a crowd of Indians. The Indians let go a hail of arrows. Tom bumped into a great Indian who was the chief. He wore a long buck skin vest and a pair of beaded moccasoins. He had a sheild of bufflo bones his beld was armed with a knife a hatchet and a toma-hawk and in it he carried a bow with on it a pack of arrows. Now I must stop telling about clothes and weapons and go on with the story. The mighty Indian rushed at Tom and threw him down. Then he leaped on Tom and was in the act of stabbing Tom with his long murderois knife but Tim Cody leaped at the Indian and knocked him down. The Indian rushed at Cody with a blood-curdling yell. But Tim before you could move whipped out his gun and fired. The chief fell dead, and Tim started to battle with the bandits but he was thrown down by a pack of howling Indians. Out went Tom's gun. But it was no use to fire for if he killed one the other pack which had surounded him would make him look like a pokepine by throwing spears into him. The Indians ran at Tom and Tim. Tom dodged a Indian and got away. But Tim rushed at an Indian and was thrown six feet in the air by the mighty Indian. Tom threw the Indian down and found him self piled on by other Indians. Suddenly a huge bandit leaped on the Indians threw them off then he picked up Tom and slung him to another man who drew knife and rushed down on Tom. But Tom leaped down to tackle him. The robber cracked Tom over the head with a gun. Tom was knocked out and the next thing that he saw that was he had been captured and he saw the sheriff sitting in a chair with a man standing gaurd over him. The war with the good men, bandits, and Indians was over. How Tom wished Tim would burst into the room. Suddenly Tom's wish came true. Into the room came Tim and six other men. Tim and the men who were the sheriffs men shot at the robbers who leaped out the windows of the building. Down the bandits fell till they reached a rope which I do not know who was the one that put it there. But it was there. As luck would have it the bandits leaped on to the rope and walked across a ledge which was jutting out from the building. Then they quickly leaped to the ground and disapeared around a corner. Tom shot at the bandits and as one got half way around the corner he stopped and suddenly crumpled to the ground and lay dead. Tom had a exciting adventure that time. Now let us stop and rest before we read.

Stop and rest! I'm going to bed!

When children speak of their elders they often refer to them as "dults" and the word sometimes carries over into their writing. A New York State mother gives us a sample of her son's prose in which he gets the word right, but misspells and misuses its relative, as follows:

ADULTS

Adults dont do anything. Adults just sit and talk and dont do a thing. Theres not anything duller in this world than adultry.

James J. Foti of Huntsville, Alabama, is a collector of children's schoolroom scribblings, but he limits himself to fourth-graders. He has stuff written by fourth-graders in Oconomowoc, Wisconsin, all the way to fourth-graders in an Air Force school in England. Among the items Mr. Foti has passed along to me is this bitter complaint from a small pessimist:

HOW I AM GOING TO SPEND MY SUMMER VACATION

I am going to go swimming all summer long. Last

summer my brothers and I wont from nine O'clock to noon. Then we go from one O'clock to six O'clock. But my brothers and I get the dirty job. The dirty job is dishes. But then we get to go swimming for the rest of the day. Sometimes I don't come home at noon so I won't have to do the dishes But I get gyped. I have to do suppers dishes. I really say thats a gyped. Not every day I get gyped. Just the days that I stay swimming I get gyped. I don't like to get gyped. But sometimes I don't care if I get gyped. Because sometimes they get gyped to. So I don't care if I get gyped with them. Because we will have to do the dishes anyway. So I don't care.

THE END

That's a real nice way to spend a summer vacation. Getting gyped. Or not getting gyped. Or not even caring.

Mr. Foti also sends an essay which, I think, may offend the sensibilities of duck hunters:

MY FAVORITE PET
We had this dog. It was a he. He was so good that my dad went out in the fall when the duck shooting was good but he did not take a gun. He waited until the shooting was all done for the day. Then we went into the marsh and got his limit of ducks that the other pople wounded.

THE
END

The Olivia Raney Library is in Raleigh, North Carolina, and some time ago I had a communication from Clyde Smith, the librarian. Clyde Smith is a lady, and she sent along a manuscript found in a book in the children's department of the library. Miss Smith said that it carried no signature, yet it is the best book review she has ever read. Here it is:

KINGS AND QUEENS

I have just finished reading "Kings and Queens" by Eleanor and Herbert Thornycroft.

One of the best stories was Henry VIII. He ruled in 1509. He had a half a dozen queens. The first was Kate of Aragon. But he got a divorce and she went. Anne Boleyn was No. 2. The live awhile. And he chopped off her head. No. 3 was Jane Seymour. A year later she jumped in bed and died. No. 4 was Anne of Cleves. A year later a Royal divorce took place. No. 5 was Catherine Howards. They got mad and off went her head. No. 6 was Catherine Parr. She was luckiest by far. This time Henry died.

Among the poetic achievements of eight-year-old Alice Fuchs of Jamaica, New York, are the following lines:

MY DEAR FATHER

If your father gets angry or very mad at you,
He's just trying to make an excellent citicen of you.

ABRAHAM LINCOLN

Lincoln was born to his parents
    One very lucky day.
He grew up very plainly,
    And had little time to play.
He studied by the fire light
    To learn geography
He was a very kind man
    And wouldn't hurt a flea.

Children have a real appreciation of climax. They usually want to be present and voting when the denouement of a story arrives. Mrs. John R. Becker of Excelsior, Minnesota, provides us with an example. One summer day Mrs. Becker found herself assigned to the job of keeping five small children entertained, three of them being her own. She decided on a "round story." She would start off with the first sentence, then one of the children would provide the second sentence, and so on around the circle, thickening the plot. So Mrs. Becker began: "Once upon a time a very pretty little girl lived high up in the mountains." Mrs. Becker now pointed to one of the children, a little girl. The child thought for only a moment, then burst forth with: "She ran out in the road and was killed."

"I think there's a special place reserved in Heaven for children's barbers and teachers," says a letter from

Fairfield, Connecticut. It is from a teacher, and she tells of the frantic time she had with her class on Columbus Day. The children were put to work writing a play commemorating the voyages of Columbus. Their teacher almost reached the limits of her endurance when a skit was handed in bearing the title, "Columbus Circumcizes the World" (I imagine it struck her as being historically incorrect).

John T. Winterich tells us of the time an author of children's books met one of his readers, an eight-year-old girl. She was obviously impressed, and asked incredulously, "Did you really write that book yourself?" Modestly, he assured her that he had. "Did you really write it all yourself?" she persisted. "Yes," he said, "I really wrote it all myself." "Well," said the child, fixing him with a beady eye, "how'd you get the lines so straight?"

I am reminded of this story time and again as I prowl through the manuscripts that have come my way. I have one before me now, a letter written by a boy in Altadena, California. The first line of the letter is fairly straight, the second line tilts a little, the third goes downhill at a greater angle, and so on — so that when I try to read the whole thing I have to twirl it like a wheel. It is a newsy letter and says:

I've got a cold right now and it feels terrible I'm much better now. Alison Nelson Debby Juile and I have gotten some kool aid which is a drink and we have made some popsicales out of it. We are going to the beach Sundy. Twinkie the cat is pregnet again. The new people next door are going 2 move in the house the 21.

Laurette Howars once published a collection of children's things including a marvelous essay:

SMELLS
Smells are things to know about. When people do good things they smell sweet. When they do bad things, they do not smell sweet at all. Dogs know about this.

An equally perceptive essay, written by a schoolgirl, was reprinted by the *Boston Evening Transcript* and follows:

PARENTS
We get our parents at so late an age that it is impossible to change their habits.

I have a niece whose father, a fowl-fancier and vegetable-grower, has to sometimes spend long periods in distant cities. The girl's mother has sent me a letter which I find noteworthy for several reasons, including its use of an expression I remember from the land of my nativity — Little Egypt in Illinois. The expression is descriptive of a physical function which, in my travels, I find has many other names among children of other localities. I know a family of Connecticut children who refer to it as "Big Dooty." And I know some younger children who refer to it as "Dwunt." There are others — a fine educational essay might be written on the subject.

But let us get at my niece's letter:

Dear Daddy,

Since you say I never write you I am going to. I know it doesn't make much since but I don't care. Your darn ginnines got out and got into the corn. We have been getting thirty to thirty-six eggs a day. Andy, Ruth and I are going to the Ball Game Friday. Their are playing Cleveland now. I am listening now and a man got on first with 2 outs and the next man got a single a man on 3rd and 1st the next guy walked and the next guy got out he hit the ball and and it went to 1 man he had to run way over and got it and then droped it picked it up threw got him out said the ump. and all the players ran out on Washingtons team. Then when Luke Easter got up he is on Cleavends side he walked and then the picther of Wash. therw a quick throw over to 1st and got him out and a whole lot of people ran out but he was out. And Your Dum Goosess DO DOED ALL OVER THE YARD. We let them out twice a day. Mother and I Cleaned out the basement and don't you drag all the stuff back either. I am playing football now and boy is it fun we are going to get lockers.

> Your Loving
> Daughter
> Jean Ann

If you failed to recognize the Little Egypt expression, it is what the dum goosess did all over the yard. And I might add that Jean Ann turned out in the end to be quite feminine; she is now a married lady, and plays no more football.

Jane Turner of Hartford tells me that her stepfather, who came from a very proper and well-to-do family, was sent away on a country vacation when he was about five years old. The first letter he wrote home was this:

Dear Mother:
> I love you very much please send me a coil of rope
> > love   Terrell
> > **XXXX OOOO**

Mrs. Leah C. Grimes of Binghamton, New York, has forwarded a biographical essay written by her son when he was nine, which was a long time ago. The essay:

ROOSEVELT

Long long ago when Columbus came, a few years before the World War Roosevelt went to Africa. He shot many kinds of anamails. He said it was very hot in that country. For a while he stade in Africa and when he came back, a year after he died.

The son of one of the most prominent authors in the South has always been a lad of imagination, and an individualist when it comes to spelling. When he was about eleven he coined a beautiful word when he said, "She is the most superfishy girl in this town." When he was five he had an attack of intestinal flu, and a nurse was engaged to attend him. The nurse overwhelmed him with numerous unwelcome enemas, and after a couple of days of this, a crude sign appeared on the boy's bedroom door. It said:

HOTEL RECTOUM
KEEP OUT

Readers of *Time* sent in a number of juvenile stories and essays after the magazine reviewed *Write Me a Poem, Baby*. A teacher took her children to the Museum of Natural History and then asked each child to write a composition. One wrote:

> Today we went to a museum. I saw a dinosaur. The dinosaur is a animal what aint got no meat on its bones.

And from Bombay came this essay, written by an eight-year-old girl:

> Once upon a time their lived a capten who loved food. His name was Bill. He married a woman called Ann. Who could cook very nicely, but he didn't love her. He only married her because she could cook. One day she died, but Bill dident mind until lunch time.

Mrs. Nathalie P. Johnston of Buffalo remembers that when she was a youngster she was composing a historical essay, and she got so excited that she wrote:

> "Who's coming?" demanded the frightened officer. "The Great Jehovah and the Continental Congress!" shouted Allen.

I have saved one of the finest items for the end of this little book. It is a little essay written by a twelve-year-old girl in Perry County, Alabama. Helen Essary came into possession of it about twenty years ago, checked it for its authenticity, and then sent it to the

Reader's Digest and *they* checked it, so it must be genuine. It was published in 1939 and follows:

TRUE GREATNESS

A person can never get True Greatness by trying for it. It is nice to have good clothes, it makes it a lot easier to act decent, but it's a sign of true greatness to act when U have not got them just as good as if U had.

Once there was a woman who had done a big washing & hung it on a line. The line broke and let it down in the mud, but she didn't say a word, only did it over again, & this time she spread it on the grass, where it could not fall.

But that night a dog with dirty feet ran over it. When she saw what was done she didn't cry a bit. All she said was: "Ain't it queer he didn't miss nothing." That was true greatness, but it is only people who have done washings that know it.

Once there was a woman that lived near a pig-pen, & when the wind blew that way it was very smelly, & at first when she went there she could not smell anything but pig, but when she lived there a while, she learned to smell the clover blossoms thru it. That was true greatness.